RESTING
in the Spirit

. . . Testimonies and Reflections on an Amazing
Little-Understood Gift of the Holy Spirit

> *"The Lord is my Shepherd*
> *I shall not want*
> *He makes me to lie down*
> *In green pastures*
> *He leads me beside quiet waters*
> *He restores my soul"*
> (Psalm 23:1-3).

Father Robert DeGrandis, S.S.J.
with Mrs. Linda Schubert

Other Books by Father DeGrandis

Renewed by the Holy Spirit
Coming to Life
Healing Through the Mass
Healing the Broken Heart
The Gift of Prophecy
The Gift of Tongues
Layperson's Manual for the Healing Ministry
To Forgive Is Divine
The Power of Healing Prayer
The Ten Commandments of Prayer
Introduction to the Catholic Charismatic Renewal
Young People's Forgiveness Prayer
Forgiveness and Inner Healing
Healing of Self-Image
(with Betty Tapscott)

All scripture quotations are from
the New International Version
unless otherwise noted

Printed in the United States of America

Contents

"Down in adoration falling
This great Sacrament we hail;
Over ancient forms of worship
newer rites of grace prevail"

Tantum Ergo
Eucharistic hymn by
St. Thomas Aquinas
c. 1320.

Foreword

My view of resting in the Spirit is not the same as the view held by a number of leaders, whom I deeply respect. Some of those opposing views have been published; others have not.

One priest who supports resting in the Spirit has pointed out that negative views are often expressed by those who have not had the experience. It has been suggested, in this case, that we may be faced with an intellectual orientation that is not balanced with real life experiences. Many people around the country, and from other countries, have encouraged me to "let the people tell their real life experiences," and thus give equal attention to the positive aspect.

I encourage the reader to join me in an opening prayer: "Holy Spirit, come. Separate us from anything that would interfere with the work You want to do in us through this book. We place ourselves under the cross of Jesus Christ and cover ourselves with the blood of Christ. We surround ourselves with the light of Christ, and say in the name of Jesus that nothing shall interfere with the Lord's purposes being accomplished in our lives. All confusion must go. All deception must cease. All distortion must stop, in Jesus' name.

"Holy Spirit, come. Wash from our minds any intellectual barriers to Your divine wisdom. Cleanse from our hearts any blockages to emotional dimensions of healing. Baptize us in the fire of Your love, and burn off the dross that encumbers our spirits. Enkindle in us a new zeal, excitement and enthusiasm for the things of God. Give us, especially, a *'Spirit of wisdom and revelation'* (Ephesians 1:17) so that we can discern Your deep truth about resting in the Spirit.

"Holy Spirit, come."

Robert DeGrandis, S.S.J.

1

The Lord Is My Shepherd, I Shall Not Want

"He tends His flock like a shepherd; He gathers the lambs in His arms and carries them close to His heart . . ." (Isaiah 40:11).

"God's Workshop . . ."
Learning From George Washington Carver

There is a story about this beloved man and how he often retired to "God's Little Workshop" to get answers to important questions. It is said that George ". . . devoutly believed that a personal relationship with the Creator of all things was the only foundation for the abundant life." Here is his story:

"I asked the Great Creator what the universe was made for.

" 'Ask for something more in keeping with that little mind of yours,' He replied.

" 'What was man made for?'

" 'Little man, you still want to know too much. Cut down the extent of your request and improve the intent.'

"Then I told the Creator I wanted to know all about the peanut. He replied that my mind was

1

too small to know all about the peanut, but He said He would give me a handful of peanuts. . . . I carried the peanuts into my laboratory and the Creator told me to take them apart and resolve them into their elements. With such knowledge as I had of chemistry and physics I set to work to take them apart. I separated the water, the fats, the oils, the gums, the resins, sugars, starches, pectoses, pentosans, amino acid. There! I had the parts of the peanuts all spread out before me.

"I looked at Him and He looked at me. 'Now, you know what the peanut is!'

" 'Why did you make the peanut?' "

It is said that with the answers to that question, George Washington Carver invented more than a hundred uses for the peanut and revived the agriculture of the South.[1]

As we begin to look for God's revelation about resting in the Spirit, I pray that each reader will go into "God's Little Workshop" and ask the Lord some questions. He tells us in Jeremiah 33:3: *"Call to Me and I will answer you and tell you great and unsearchable things you do not know."*

Introduction

"Resting in the Spirit" is a controversial topic in our day and time, widely publicized in the press and often discussed in reference to the charismatic renewal. Like praying in tongues, this experience of resting on the floor during prayer has caught man's attention. Little is written about it; much is still unknown. It is somewhat virgin territory, especially in the Catholic community.

Because it is making its appearance and having its effects, I want to open up communication and encourage dialogue. I want to examine what I believe is a movement of the Holy Spirit in our day.

Resting in the Spirit is most probably a charismatic gift, at least in part. There seems to be a dual charism: The charism in some people, in whom the power is so strong that most individuals will go down when they pray over them; and the charism in some recipients, who are so open to receive that they will fall under the power when anyone prays.

The *Second Vatican Council Dogmatic Constitution on the Church,* paragraph 12, in speaking of the charismatic gifts, says:

> ". . . whether they are the more outstanding or the more simple and widely diffused, they are to be received with thanksgiving and consolation, for they are exceedingly suitable and useful to the needs of the Church."

What we want to do in this book is begin to explore the "suitability and usefulness" of this gift, and "receive it with thanksgiving."

As I begin to consider guidelines for the use of such a charism as resting in the Spirit, I am reminded of a time I was listening to an expert on discernment and decision making. It was said that ideas should not only come down from the top, but also up from the bottom. The wisdom of the people needs to be heard and discerned. There is always a tendency when something unusual in the Spirit comes, to categorically deny it without giving ear to the people's experience.

I also firmly believe that in the discernment process, it is important to look at the fruit of the experiences as seen in the ministries of such men as Father Ralph Di-Orio, Father Edward McDonough and others in a full-time healing ministry. The discernment of people with integrity and esteem has great value.

And finally, those of us who are Catholic look to the Church for guidance and discernment, recognizing it as a God-given authority.

What we want to do is: explore the wisdom of others in the healing ministry who have themselves rested in the Spirit; listen to what some health care professionals have to say; hear the testimonies of lay men and women from all walks of life. We will also look at some of the pastoral problems with resting in the Spirit and suggest some preliminary guidelines. This is not a book of answers. It is, rather, a vehicle through which I hope to stimulate some healthy and balanced discussion that will lay some of the foundation for future pastoral and theological direction on resting in the Spirit.

A number of health care professionals and researchers made some suggestions concerning the manner in which the material is presented. They suggested that we:

* Have well written stories from people who are open, who ask questions, who want to report and not convince.
* Tell their attitude, relate the sense of meaning the experience had for them.
* Collect experience.

I am grateful to the many contributors who shared their hearts so openly and freely. Their responses are valuable, and appreciated.

In a survey of 200 individuals who have on a number of occasions rested in the Spirit (see Appendix and the end of the first six sections), the most common feeling shared was a sense of being "loved and cared for" by

God. It is for this reason that I present the material within the context of the familiar Twenty-Third Psalm. This portion of scripture powerfully portrays the sense of the Lord's loving, caring ministry. This sense of being loved and cared for is foundational to the ministry of healing. I concur with Msgr. Walsh in *Keep the Flame Alive*[2] that resting in the Spirit finds its place within the general framework of the healing ministry. As we get in touch with the Lord's love nature we open to wholeness in every area of our lives.

"And so we know and rely on the love God has for us. God is love. Whoever lives in love lives in God, and God in him" (1 John 4:16-17).

My first personal experience with resting in the Spirit occurred in a Kathryn Kuhlman service in 1971. I remember lying on the floor and feeling a deep peace, and an awareness of God's tremendous power. Since that time I have rested on the floor at least 50 times. If I counted the times I have rested in the Spirit while sitting in a chair receiving prayer, it would be closer to 75 or 100 times. Almost always when I am receiving inner healing, I rest in the Spirit.

One of the best resting experiences I ever had was in Brazil after a long hard day of ministry. I was exhausted, and someone offered to rest me in the Spirit. After a short while resting with the Lord I got up totally refreshed and renewed. It was fantastic! Sometimes if I am experiencing stress prior to a workshop I will have someone rest me in the Spirit. I may rest 20 minutes or so, and then be ready to go, more sensitive, open and able to know the direction the Lord wants me to take in that particular ministry.

In 1972 at Notre Dame, when I was called up to pray

on a team with Francis MacNutt, I had my first experience resting another person in the Spirit. When I asked Barbara Shlemon to examine the person who had fallen, she indicated that the individual was "just resting in the Spirit." It was something I had never seen.

As time went on and I moved into a full-time healing ministry in the charismatic renewal, resting in the Spirit developed into a powerful avenue of healing, especially in large groups where there was no time for extended individual prayer. I began to hear stories of the Lord doing very deep healing in amazingly brief periods of time, as people rested quietly in seats or on the floor during healing services. Individuals who had been in counseling for years, with no significant growth, received deep healing and breakthrough in personal growth while resting in the Spirit.

It has been my experience that one of the most powerful ways of helping people receive healing and experience growth in prayer is through resting in the Spirit. I used to teach courses on prayer, but now with these courses I also help people open to the experience of resting in the Spirit. Sometimes on all-day workshops or weekend retreats, I will pray to rest the participants in the Spirit prior to the teaching at the beginning of the retreat, in the middle, and at the end of the retreat. This experience opens them to receive from the Lord more effectively than any other method I have discovered. Some of the deepest healings have come to people on retreats where they have rested in the Spirit on several occasions.

Today, as I travel across the United States and to many other countries conducting leadership training and healing services in a full-time ministry, I see countless hundreds of participants rest in the Spirit — even bishops!

One bishop in Chile came up to me to receive prayer and rested deeply in the Spirit. I heard years later that he had a deep, mystical experience. Another bishop in a Latin country, who rested twice in the Spirit, expressed great pleasure with the experience. Yet another bishop, a saintly and holy man, rested in the Spirit on a priest retreat. It is fascinating how many bishops have rested in the Spirit.

Initially, when the charismatic experience emerged in the Church, some bishops and priests repressed it, saying there would be no prayer groups, or prayer groups but no tongues, or tongues but no laying on of hands, etc. Many of them changed their minds after the national bishops' statement in 1969 which indicated that prayer groups must be allowed because they bear good fruit.

Yet there are those who still do not even fully accept the Vatican Council. Probably it will take 50 or 100 years for some people to accept it. So we can't expect resting in the Spirit, this new phenomenon, to be totally accepted immediately. But I think what we are trying to do in this book is bring it out in the open to be discussed and to provoke discussion.

One of the main comments I hear when I minister is, "Father, you are the first to give us a detailed explanation of resting in the Spirit." I remember as early as 1974, people in prayer groups were falling down under the power of the Spirit as they praised the Lord. Many didn't understand it, and were fearful.* Lack of understanding has led to confusion, misunderstanding and abuse. The subject needs to be opened up for discussion. We can't turn our backs on it, or repress it.

I'm not denying that there are pastoral problems. What I believe we need to do, is get some pastoral an-

*See question 3 on page 19.

swers for pastoral problems, while not quenching the Spirit. John in the epistles says, *"test the spirits"* (1 John 4:1), and this is what we are trying to do: test them first for authenticity and then for practicality.

Some of the commentators who criticize resting in the Spirit have never had the experience, according to my research. I feel it is misleading for a person who has not experienced something as subjective as resting in the Spirit to come against it with just intellectual arguments. It would be akin to having a man write a book on the joy of having a baby. No man could adequately describe the joy of pregnancy because it is a woman's subjective experience.

Yet we can thank those who have argued negatively about it, because they force those of us who look positively upon this experience to give reason for our faith. The negativity I have encountered has moved me to take a deeper, more careful look at the stand that I and others in the full-time healing ministry take on this powerful and sensitive topic.

We live in a violent society; we have violent entertainment in movies and on television — murder, rape, shooting, stabbing, bludgeoning, etc. Resting in the Spirit (or slaying in the Spirit) is "sweet violence," so to speak — the overwhelming power of the Holy Spirit. Yet some people react negatively. Some people who see murder and rape and mutilation and brutality accept that input, but get upset at seeing people fall under the power of the Holy Spirit. That doesn't make too much sense. It is said that by the time an American is 18 years old he has seen 100,000 instances of violence on television. One famous protestant evangelist has said, "We watch on television in our day things that would have been unthinkable to see ten years ago. We are being lulled into paganism."

And, our people are being lured into cults. Countless thousands of Catholics have been drawn into religious cults and a variety of para-psychological movements as a means of experiencing God, finding their inner selves, or finding happiness. The *Vatican Report on Sects, Cults and New Religious Movements* comments in paragraph 2.1.3: "The sects appear to offer: a gratifying religious experience, being saved, conversion: room for feelings and emotions, for spontaneity (e.g., in religious celebrations). . . ."[3] The loss of our people to these cults is a challenge to us to make room for satisfying religious experience in the Catholic Church.

We have a God who wants us to experience His love nature. He is also a God of surprise, who calls us at times to risky living.

Some years ago at a national charismatic convention at Notre Dame University, Ralph Martin commented that we in the renewal have to be careful in that we are becoming too respectable. He stated that the renewal has a prophetic function. It challenges us to change, and grow.

Everywhere I go, I hear pastors saying, "We need something . . . people are hungry . . . people are searching." They are faced with the need, and a sense of powerlessness to bring about change.

In an article in *New Covenant,* Father James Hughes shares about the need for spiritual formation in the youth of his parish, and the manner in which God met this need:

". . . I began with a small group of young people who agreed to go on a retreat. At the penance service, the presence of God grew so strong that almost all of the young people were overcome by the Spirit. They were called to deep conversion. Many were baptized in the Spirit and began to speak in tongues. . . . Frankly, some problems developed as we made some changes . . . yet we carried on. Soon I was confronted with a formidable challenge — a huge confirmation class of about 100 young people. I threw out the texts and conducted a Life in the Spirit seminar, trusting in the guidance of the Holy Spirit to keep me on course. The class responded. . . . As soon as we decided not to play it safe with what we had, God answered immediately. . . .

"The heart of the program is conversion. I emphasize the charismatic gifts and baptism in the Holy Spirit because these things lead to conversion — a change in mind and heart. These kids need Jesus. The charismatic experience makes His love and power obvious. . . . What is the secret of change? The Lord is in charge. The hearts of young people are changed when we all step aside and allow Him to work."[4]

The need for conversion is as true for an 80 year old as it is for an eight year old. Conversion means change, and change is often risky, frightening and troublesome.

In every story shared in this book, you will find the seeds of conversion being watered in the hearts of the people. Every story is an example of surrender to the ministry of the Holy Spirit.

Pope Paul VI in his *Encyclical on Evangelism in the Modern World,* Article 75, page 51, states:

"It is in the 'consolation of the Holy Spirit' that the Church increases. The Holy Spirit is the soul of the Church. It is He who explains to the faithful the deep meaning of the teaching of Jesus and of His mystery. It is the Holy Spirit who,

today just as at the beginning of the Church, acts
in every evangelizer who allows himself to be possessed and led by Him.''

Father Matthew Linn made an interesting observation
one time that there is a ''pre-evangelization'' and ''post-
evangelization'' aspect of resting in the Spirit. For those
non-Christians or indifferent Christians with no deep al-
legiance to the Lord, ''resting'' often opens their hearts
to hear the word of God. The post-evangelization aspect
of resting is for those who have accepted the Lord and
are bearing fruit. Resting draws them deeper into prayer,
increasing the gift of contemplation. The need for conversion is on-going, for all of us.

A handful of Catholic charismatics at Duquesne University in 1967 allowed themselves to be possessed and
led by the Holy Spirit. After they received the baptism
in the Spirit and began to pray in tongues, they risked
their reputations to tell their remarkable story to a church
that did not accept the gift of tongues. The Spirit of God,
in giving dramatic gifts, certainly gets the attention of
both hot and cold Catholics. He seems to be wooing the
faithful and unfaithful alike with a new brand of loving.

Definitions

It might be helpful to start at a very elementary position and first define ''religious experience.'' And for
those readers who are new to the concept of resting in
the Spirit, we will share some definitions of the experience from several perspectives. And then we will touch
upon the difference between ''spontaneous'' and ''ministered'' resting.

RELIGIOUS EXPERIENCE: A "sensation and feeling level" awareness of God that generates a spontaneous response. Often it is accompanied by a revelation, inspiration, visions and conversion.

RESTING IN THE SPIRIT: The experience of falling back on the floor during prayer is sometimes called "Overwhelmed by the Spirit," "Falling Under the Power," "Dormition," "Slain in the Spirit," or simply "The Blessing." While I prefer to call the experience "Resting in the Spirit," there will be a number of quotes referring to "Slain" in the Spirit. The terms will be interchangeable.

There doesn't seem to be a simple description that covers the whole experience. In my book *Laypersons Manual for the Healing Ministry,* I state:

"Seemingly while we are resting in the Spirit the physical and the psychological functions are slowed down and the spiritual sensitivity is intensified in relationship with the Lord. . . ."[5]

In the following definitions we find some agreement about a yielding, surrendering, giving way or quieting of the activity and senses of the physical body so that God can manifest Himself more clearly to the inner nature.

Francis MacNutt in *The Power to Heal* states: "So far as I can see, it is the power of the Spirit so filling a person with a heightened inner awareness that the body's energy fades away until it cannot stand."[6]

Father George Montague in *Catholic Charismatic* magazine says: ". . . .one is overcome by a deep sense of well-being which momentarily relaxes the person in such a way that he surrenders the central motor control and swoons or falls limp."[7]

Father Ralph DiOrio comments: ". . . it is part of the

gift of healing, a direct touching of the innermost being by an infilling of God's love and peace."[8]

Kenneth Hagin in *Why Do People Fall Under the Power?* says: "When the natural comes into contact with the supernatural, something has to give."[9]

Morton Kelsey comments in *Discernment:* ". . . they generally describe a sense of holy power or energy flowing in, which makes them relax and fall. . . ."[10]

I also like the simple description given by a pediatrician: "It seems to be the outward evidence of releasing the inner self to the Lord."

Father Ted Dobson prefers to completely separate the act of falling from an evaluation of the cause of the fall, and simply refers to the experience as "The falling phenomenon." Referring to all of the many descriptions, he states: ". . . these names only begin to give us a clue to what is actually happening . . . we will refer to it as 'the falling phenomenon,' not only because falling to the ground is the one thing that is common to all the different forms of the experience, but also because it is a term that is value-free, that does not presuppose a cause to the experience."[11]

Father Thomas Keating in *Open Mind, Open Heart,* states: ". . . you feel a mild suspension of your ordinary sense faculties and you slip to the floor. If people have never experienced this kind of prayer before, they go down with great delight and stay down as long as they can."[12]

An analogy that I sometimes use is that of lying in the sun. People simply lie in the sun, let the sun come upon them and relax them. Resting in the Spirit is akin to letting the sun of the Holy Spirit inside. As they rest they will in many cases have a direct encounter with the Lord. The Lord will then do much healing. They will sense His love, experience Him talking to them, and simply rest in His presence.

Msgr. Vincent Walsh refers to the experience as "dormition,"[13] which is a word that suggests sleep, and hints at some sort of kinship with the experience of ecstasy spoken of in the writings of the saints. But it isn't sleep. The person resting is aware of people acting and speaking in his environment, and therefore it is different from sleep. They can hear what is going on, but could care less. Their energy seems to be caught up with the Lord. It is like being intently engrossed in a TV program in a noisy, crowded room. A person is focused directly on the TV and tuned out to the people. While resting in the Spirit, the person is intensely focused on the Lord.

SPONTANEOUS AND MINISTERED RESTING: Another definition that might be helpful is that which would distinguish between "spontaneous" resting and "ministered" resting.

Spontaneous resting: Falling down under the power of the Spirit with no intermediary, as in the middle of a prayer meeting or in private prayer.

Ministered resting (Might also be referred to as cooperative or induced resting): Resting that may occur as a result of prayers to remove barriers to the Holy Spirit, or music, or teaching or the physical action of raising the arms in surrender, or expressed desire to rest, after people are anointed at a healing service or prayer meeting and then rest in the Spirit.

"Within Your temple, O God, we meditate on Your unfailing love" (Psalm 48:9).

Testimonies

"21 Cigars . . ." Sister Linda Koontz Shares a Special Story

"I met Christa when she was about 71 years old. Her uncle brought her to America from Copenhagen, Denmark, when she was in her early 20's and then died when they were on a train and left her all alone. She stayed in this country and had an unhappy life. She made an unfortunate marriage and experienced a lot of suffering and grief. Because of her loneliness and lack of friends and being unable to return to her own country, she became an alcoholic. Christa was an abandoned woman, lonely and distraught.

"A sister at my convent befriended her, but could not handle the demands the woman made. One night about 1 a.m. Christa called the sister in my convent. She was in a bad state and needed immediate help. The nun was so exhausted that she asked me to visit the lady. I went and found her sitting at a table with a loaded gun and an empty whiskey bottle. She was intoxicated, and in such deep despair that she felt she could not face life anymore. Her solution for the despair and anguish was to kill herself.

"I did not know what to do, so I called a nurse-friend from my prayer group. The nurse came and she didn't know what to do either. I took Christa into the bedroom and sat her on the bed. I saw it was no use trying to talk to her, so in my heart I asked, 'Lord, what can I do?' The thought came to me, 'Pray for her.' I was very new at that time in praying for people, and did not know what approach to take. The words came to me, 'Jesus, help.' When I cried those words out loud, Christa fell back onto her bed as if in a faint. The nurse thought maybe she had

15

a heart attack. I knew very little at this point about resting in the Spirit. I had never seen it happen. But she appeared to be sleeping peacefully and relaxed, so we decided not to disturb her. I stayed the night.

"When she woke up the next morning Christa was completely sober and full of joy. She said, 'I feel so good. I know God loves me.' While she was asleep, Jesus had come to her. I prayed with her to surrender her life to Jesus Christ. She was baptized in the Holy Spirit and prayed in tongues. Within the week we began scripture study together. Her whole personality changed.

"The first morning after her rest she said to me, 'I don't feel like having my cigar today.' She smoked 21 cigars a day. Christa was set free from alcohol and cigar smoking. She had owned her own cigar factory in Copenhagen from the time she was a young woman. That's why there was a cigar habit.

"Whereas before she was abusive to people and very belligerent, she became known for her sweet nature. She began attending prayer meetings and reached out to make friends with all kinds of people. Within a short time she was giving her testimony at the prayer meetings. She was baptized and made her first communion, and witnessed to many people about God's love and God's power.

"A few years after her conversion it was discovered that she had cancer. She peacefully and patiently endured the suffering and encouraged others to trust God as she trusted God. My friend was with her when she died. Although she was supposed to be in a coma, Christa sat up in her sickbed with a radiant smile and held out her arms as if someone was receiving her.

"In her casket she looked like a young woman; all the years of suffering and ravages of cancer had left her body. People could not stop remarking on the youthful beauty of her face.

"Instead of spending her days in despair and depression she read scripture, received the sacraments and interceded for people who were suffering. She especially interceded for the work of evangelism through my ministry. Christa was a great gift in my life. I can only say that God accomplished this tremendous conversion and grace through her experience of resting in the Spirit."[14]

"Waves of Grace . . ." Billy's Story

"It was not easy for me to rest in the Spirit, for I was doubtful of its validity. But this is how our Lord finally led me to believe. I had seen Father DeGrandis and had a hard time with the whole thing — healing, singing, even praising. About a year later, after a few prayer meetings and receiving prayer on several occasions, a good friend took me to hear a talk given by Father DeGrandis' sister, Dorothea. Soon after that experience this same friend persuaded me to hear Father DeGrandis again. I must confess that I still had some doubts. It was the feast day of Mary, so I asked for her intercession. About ten of us from our prayer group had gone to the afternoon meeting. After the talk, Father DeGrandis asked for those who wanted to be blessed with oil to come forward. People started falling over, one after the other. When Father was praying over the person next to me, he reached over and touched my little pinky finger which was held up in the air. In a moment I felt myself going over. I thought to myself, 'Is this it?' Well, it was.

"While I lay there resting, it felt like waves of grace washing me from head to foot. The music group began singing a song about Mary (which confirmed her intercession on my behalf). I felt wonderful! When I got up,

all of my friends said, 'Look at Billy! He really got it!'
I guess I was beaming. What really convinced me of the
validity of the experience was a total release of all fear.*
In its place was a belated recognition of God's presence
in all the other times I'd received prayer.''

"When Did I Pull Those Teeth?" Barbara's Story

"The day after I had two teeth pulled, my neighbor,
Muriel, invited me to a special evening Mass with Father
DeGrandis. I had heard a little about him from Muriel but
I had never been to a healing service, nor did I know anything about the charismatic renewal. I had never heard of,
or witnessed, resting in the Spirit. When Mass was over
I followed Muriel and Father DeGrandis to the back of
the church, thinking they were leaving. However, at the
back they stopped and turned around, facing me. Muriel
said, 'Barbara, if you want the Holy Spirit to come into
your life, lift up your hands and invite Him in.' As I responded, Father DeGrandis anointed me on the forehead
and started praying. I was instantly engulfed from head
to toe in a tremendous loving warmth. Although my eyes
were closed, I seemed surrounded by a brilliant light. For
some time I was not aware of anything or anyone around
me. When I gradually became aware of voices I still didn't
want to open my eyes because I felt so wonderful in the
warmth and light. When I opened my eyes I saw people
lying on the floor all down the aisle. This was the first time
I was really aware that I was on the floor too!
"I went back to the dentist a few days later to have
the stitches removed. When he looked in my mouth he
pulled the light closer and looked again. He kept exam-

*Note in question 5 on page 39 the kinds of healing men have received
while resting in the Spirit.

18

ining my mouth. Finally he spoke. 'When did I pull those teeth?' 'Four days ago,' I responded. 'This is remarkable. Your gums are healed as if I pulled them two or three years ago!' "

AREN'T YOU GLAD WE ASKED? . . .
statistics from survey

Two hundred individuals (148 women and 52 men) were surveyed about resting in the Spirit in workshops around the country. The majority of the people surveyed had previously rested in the Spirit from 3 to 20 times. Seventy-three of them had been in the renewal 3-7 years, 42 had been in the renewal 7-10 years and 50 were seasoned veterans with over 10 years in the renewal. Tabulations of the responses to the questionnaire will begin here and continue at the end of the next five chapters. How would you have answered these questions?

1. Was there an explanation of resting in the Spirit prior to the experience?

Yes	62%
No	31%
Not answered	7%

2. Were you encouraged to rest in the Spirit?

Yes	62%
No	36%
Not answered	2%

3. Were you frightened when you rested in the Spirit the first time?

Yes	25%
No	72%
Not answered	3%

(Generally, the men indicated less fear than the women. Eighteen percent of the men admitted fear compared with 28% of the women.)

4. Were you surprised at your first experience?

Yes	69%
No	28%
Not answered	3%

(The women's answers reflected a little more surprise than the men's answers at 71% compared with 63% of the men.)

. . . to be continued

Review of Key Points

* The present-day experience of falling on the floor during prayer is generally called "resting in the Spirit."

* Resting can occur both spontaneously and cooperatively.

* Resting can be a charism active in both the leader and the recipient.

* Resting is generally considered to be a part of the healing ministry.

* During prayer a power seems to flow in, causing physical energy to fade.

* Feeling loved, cared for and empowered by God are commonly expressed values of resting in the Spirit.

* Catholics are generally hungry for satisfying religious experience.

* Because resting in the Spirit is new to most Catholics, and controversial, it needs to be opened up for theological and pastoral discussion and discernment.

* We are all being called to on-going conversion.

* Sometimes God uses surprising ways to catch man's attention.

Prayer

Heavenly Father, draw me closer to You and open my ears to hear what You have to say about resting in the Spirit. Give me a teachable spirit, an open mind, wisdom and discernment.

Father, I want to lie in the sun of Your love and allow You to capture my full attention. Let me experience on-going conversion and breakthrough in personal growth. Remove from me, as You did from Christa, any and all addictions. If there is abusiveness in my nature, convert it to sweetness. Release me, as you did Billy, from any unknown fears. Bring me, as You did Barbara, into physical health. And help me, as You did Father James Hughes, to grow beyond simply playing it safe, that I can make Your love and power obvious in the world. Thank You, heavenly Father, in Jesus' name. Amen.

"The Lord will guide you always; He will satisfy your needs . . . you will be like a well-watered garden . . ." (Isaiah 58:11).

21

2

He Makes Me to Lie Down in Green Pastures

"Come, let us bow down in worship, let us kneel before the Lord our Maker; for He is our God and we are the people of His pasture, the flock under His care . . ." (Psalm 95:6-7).

Foundations in Scripture

As we come increasingly in contact with the phenomenon of resting in the Spirit, one of the first questions that arises is, "Where do we find it in scripture?" Are there biblical parallels or similarities? Morton Kelsey states:

> "There was obviously nothing in biblical times exactly similar to a modern service in which people come forward, are touched and fall down: on the other hand, there are many references in the Old and New Testament to people who fall before God and seemed to be struck down by His Spirit."[15]

There are scripture references to falling down in the presence of God, both voluntarily and involuntarily, in both positive and negative contexts.

I. Voluntary Prostration

    A. In Thanksgiving. Falling before God in worship and gratitude. Luke 17:15-16, where the leper was healed, is an example. *"One of them, when he saw he was healed, came back, praising God in a loud voice. He threw himself at Jesus' feet and thanked Him. . . ."*

    B. In a Deep Burden of Prayer. *"For this reason I kneel before the Father, from whom His whole family in heaven and on earth derives its name. I pray that out of His glorious riches He may strengthen you with power through His Spirit in your inner being . . ."* (Ephesians 3:14-16).

       Also in Matthew 26:39: Jesus, in Gethsemane *". . . fell with His face to the ground and prayed, 'My Father, if it is possible, may this cup be taken from me. Yet not as I will, but as You will."*

II. Involuntary Prostration

    A. Spiritual Clash
       "About noon . . . as I was on the road, I saw a light from heaven, brighter than the sun, blazing around me and my companions. We all fell to the ground, and I heard a voice saying to me . . . 'Saul, Saul, why do you persecute me? . . .' " (Acts 26:13-14).

       Jeremiah 46:15: *"Why will your warriors be laid low? They cannot stand, for the Lord will push them down."*

       When Jesus was arrested, Judas brought the soldiers to Gethsemane. John 18:4-6: *"Jesus, knowing all that was going to happen to Him,*

went out and asked them, 'Who is it you want?'
'Jesus of Nazareth,' they replied. 'I am He,'
Jesus said. . . . When Jesus said, 'I am He,' they
all drew back and fell to the ground."

B. Overwhelmed by His Presence in an Ecstatic Way.
   In the Old Testament at the dedication of
Solomon's temple. Second Chronicles 5:13-14:
"The trumpeters and singers joined in unison,
as with one voice, to give praise and thanks to
the Lord. Accompanied by trumpets, cymbals
and other instruments, they raised their voices
in praise to the Lord. . . . Then the temple of
the Lord was filled with a cloud, and the priests
could not perform their service because of the
cloud, for the glory of the Lord filled the tem-
ple of God."

Daniel 10:8-9: "So I was left alone, gazing at
this great vision; I had no strength left, my face
turned deathly pale and I was helpless. Then I
heard him speaking, and as I listened to him, I
fell into a deep sleep, my face to the ground."

Ezekiel 1:28: ". . . This was the appearance of
the likeness of the glory of the Lord. When I saw
it, I fell downward, and I heard the voice of one
speaking."

Ezekiel 43:3: "The vision I saw was like the vi-
sion I had seen when he came to destroy the city
and like the visions I had seen by the Kebar
River, and I fell face down."

John on Patmos was caught up in ecstasy when
he saw *"One like the Son of Man." "When I*
saw Him I fell down at His feet as though
dead . . ." (Revelation 1:17).

24

When God sends a man flat on his face (or his back), why does He do it? Father John Hampsch, C.M.F., suggests a few possible reasons:

"With Peter (Acts 10:10) and Paul (Acts 9:4), the purpose was to ensure that the person receiving the revelation was impacted with the awareness of God's very direct involvement. With Daniel (Daniel 10:8-9), it was to convince him of the truth of a vision and prophecy . . . on Patmos, John was overpowered when he received the revelation that became the whole Book of Revelation (1:17). With the soldiers at the tomb (Matthew 28:4), God showed His overcoming power.

"God can cause His friends and His enemies to fall to the ground, with different purposes in each case. One case shows that the human power will not overcome God's power; the other case, with friends, is that God's power will enhance human powers or talents. The main purpose of this particular phenomenon is to manifest the power of God, as suggested in Acts 1:8: *'You will receive power when the Holy Spirit comes upon you.'* The power could be expressed possibly by being overpowered by God, as the soldiers were overpowered by the presence of Jesus and slain in the Spirit at the moment they tried to arrest Him (John 18:6). In other instances the power is expressed actively by way of insight into the nature and goodness of God, inner healing, bestowing inner peace, etc."[16]

". . . Jesus came to them and said, 'All authority in heaven and on earth has been given to me' " (Matthew 28:18).

"Consider the Eloquence . . ."
St. Augustine's Story and Other References to the Saints

Father John Hampsch tracked down an interesting story told by St. Augustine in *The City of God:*

"There were seven brothers and three sisters of a noble family of the Cappadocian Caesarea, who were cursed by their mother, a new-made widow, on account of some wrong they had done her, and which she bitterly resented, and who were visited with so severe a punishment from Heaven, that all of them were seized with a hideous shaking in all their limbs. Unable, while presenting this loathsome appearance, to endure the eyes of their fellow-citizens, they wandered over almost the whole Roman world, each following his own direction. Two of them came to Hippo, a brother and a sister, Paulus and Palladia, already known in many other places by the fame of their wretched lot.

"Now it was about fifteen days before Easter when they came, and they came daily to church, and especially to the relics of the most glorious Stephen, praying that God might now be appeased, and restore their former health. There, and wherever they went, they attracted the attention of every one. Some who had seen them elsewhere, and knew the cause of their trembling, told others as occasion offered. Easter arrived, and on the Lord's day, in the morning, when there was now a large crowd present, and the young man was holding the bars of the holy place where the relics were, and praying, suddenly he fell down, and lay precisely as if asleep, but not trembling as he was wont to do even in sleep. All present were aston-

26

ished. Some were alarmed, some were moved with pity; and while some were for lifting him up, others prevented them, and said they should rather wait and see what would result. And behold! he rose up, and trembled no more, for he was healed, and stood quite well, scanning those who were scanning him.

"Who then refrained himself from praising God? The whole church was filled with the voices of those who were shouting and congratulating him. Then they came running to me, where I was sitting ready to come into the church. One after another they throng in, the last comer telling me as news what the first had told me already; and while I rejoiced and inwardly gave God thanks, the young man himself also enters, with a number of others, falls at my knees, is raised up to receive my kiss. We go in to the congregation: the church was full, and ringing with the shouts of joy, 'Thanks to God! Praised be God!' every one joining and shouting on all sides, 'I have healed the people,' and then with still louder voice shouting again. Silence being at last obtained, the customary lessons of the divine scriptures were read. And when I came to my sermon, I made a few remarks suitable to the occasion and the happy and joyful feeling, not desiring them to listen to me, but rather to consider the eloquence of God in this divine work.

"The man dined with us, and gave us a careful account of his own, his mother's, and his family's calamity. Accordingly, on the following day, after delivering my sermon, I promised that next day I would read his narrative to the people.

And when I did so, the third day after Easter Sunday, I made the brother and sister both stand on the steps of the raised place from which I used to speak; and while they stood there their pamphlet was read. The whole congregation, men and women alike, saw the one standing without any unnatural movement, the other trembling in all her limbs; so that those who had not before seen the man himself saw in his sister what the divine compassion had removed from him. In him they saw matter of congratulation, in her subject for prayer.

"Meanwhile, their pamphlet being finished, I instructed them to withdraw from the gaze of the people; and I had begun to discuss the whole matter somewhat more carefully, when lo! as I was proceeding, other voices are heard from the tomb of the martyr, shouting new congratulations. My audience turned around, and began to rush to the tomb. The young woman, when she had come down from the steps where she had been standing, went to pray at the holy relics, and no sooner had she touched the bars than she, in the same way as her brother, collapsed, as if falling asleep, and rose up cured. While, then, we were asking what had happened, and what occasioned this noise of joy, they came into the basilica where we were, leading her from the martyr's tomb in perfect health. Then, indeed, such a shout of wonder rose from men and women together, that the exclamations and the tears seemed like never to come to an end."[17]

E. Allison Peers quotes the experience of St. Teresa, in the *Complete Works of St. Teresa of Jesus:*

". . . the Lord takes this little bird and puts it into the nest where it may repose. . . . While seeking God in this way, the soul becomes conscious that it is fainting almost completely away, in a kind of swoon, with an exceeding great and sweet delight. . . . In this condition all outward strength vanishes, while the strength of soul increases . . ."[18]

Francis MacNutt in *The Power to Heal* brings some additional understanding about the roots of resting in the Spirit in the tradition of the Church.

"Teresa's experience resulted, of course, from her great union with God — she was an extraordinary saint; but I also remembered what happened to ordinary people through the ministry of John Tauler, a German Dominican preacher of the 14th Century.

"I had read his story when I was a novice at Winona, Minnesota, back in 1950, and it always stayed with me. John was a famous preacher in Cologne, and one day he was talking in the sacristy to a layman who had been taking notes on his sermons. When John pressed him to say what he thought of John's preaching, the layman was very reluctant to speak; but finally he was pressed to say that he felt John was like the Pharisees who operated more out of the pride of intellect than by the light of the Spirit. John was, naturally, cut to the heart. After an interior struggle, he offered to take the unusual action (especially for that era) of submitting himself to the layman's direction. This man told John to stop preaching and to pray and study for a time. When John did this, his Do-

minican brothers thought he was becoming un-
balanced and ridiculed him."[19]

As the story goes, John Tauler had a powerful encounter with the Lord (apparently while resting in the
Spirit), and he was " . . . gifted with clear perceptions
of matters that had before been very strange to him."[20]
The layman told him that he had, for the first time, been
touched by the Lord, and that from now on, his teaching would come from "God the Holy Ghost." When he
returned to preaching, it was with such great effect that
forty men rested in the Spirit.

Francis MacNutt continues:

"From my remembrance of having read this
account from the traditional spiritual literature of
the Roman Catholic Church, I was helped not to
be surprised by the novelty of it all, but to see that
such extraordinary phenomena could happen to
ordinary people. . . ."

Francis MacNutt further commented that the story
of Tauler illustrated the possible value of external pub-
licity, the benefit to ministry, and the need for the minister of resting to be infilled by the Holy Spirit.[21]

Around the World in Pentecostal Circles

Resting in the Spirit occurred in the ministry of John
Wesley, the founder of Methodism; it occurred with reviv-
alist Charles Finney and became a regular part of histor-
ical pentecostal churches. Then it began more or less
frequently in mainline Christian churches. In every age of
the church there seems to be somewhat similar manifestations of God.

Stanley Frodsham in *With Signs Following* gives many examples from around the world:

New England, 1870's, speaking of a young, high-spirited girl who witnessed the healing of her invalid sister, ". . . she fell prostrate under the hand of God, and when she rose she had yielded her heart to God."

Arkansas, 1879 — A young man testifies: "Sometimes in the services and sometimes when alone in prayer, I would fall prostrate under God's mighty power."

Azusa Street, Los Angeles, 1906 — "As the people came they would fall under the power, and the whole city was stirred."

India, 1905 — "Some fell as they saw a great light. While the fire of God burned, the members of the body of sin, pride, love of the world, selfishness, uncleanness, etc., passed before them. . . ."

Pennsylvania, 1907 — ". . . suddenly he fell prostrate to the platform and was immediately baptized in the Spirit, speaking in tongues."

Canada, 1907 — "For some time I lay prostrate at His blessed feet, gazing on Him, and so enraptured with His unspeakable glory I felt lost to every being and everything but Himself alone. He touched the temple He wanted to occupy and moved it in His own way."

Ohio, 1908 — ". . . I saw what could not be less than from 50-75 people prostrated at one time under the power of God."

South America, 1908 — ". . . a brother who

31

had been many years in the church but was wholly useless as a Christian, arose and asked for prayer. He had scarcely expressed the request when he fell as if knocked by a blow. Whereas formerly he was unable to pray, now the words rushed from his mouth in a torrent . . . from that day forward he became a man of prayer and power."

South America, 1909 — ". . . four vain young ladies (three of whom were in the choir) fell to the floor under the power of the Spirit . . . one arose and spoke with power and conviction."

South America, 1909 — ". . . a daze seemed to rest on the people. Some were unable to rise after the opening prayer which had been like 'the sound of many waters,' and all were filled with wonder. . . . These amazing scenes brought constantly increasing crowds of curious ones and the congregation grew by leaps and bounds. . . ."

China, 1914 — the story of a blind woman: "After praying a short time she was filled with the Spirit. She knew nothing of the English language but the Holy Spirit soon began to speak through her in English and the first word was 'worship.' While prostrate on the floor the Spirit of God spoke this word through her perhaps a score of times. Other words followed in English, among them the word, 'HIS.' Then the word, 'REST.' And the very expression suggested rest."[22]

Resting in the Spirit occurred regularly in the ministry of the protestant healing evangelist, Kathryn Kuhlman. She comments about people's response to the power of God in her book, *A Glimpse Into Glory:*

"... these bodies are not wired for so much power.... They are not geared for heaven.... When a person comes face to face with Him, it is too much for his physical body.... God is alive.... He is the very essence of power. He is not just the author of power, He is all power.... When you consider the Holy Spirit can heal a sick body without anyone touching that body — that's power. Therefore, isn't it logical to believe this body can stand only so much of that power before it is short circuited?"

She relates a story about a professor of theology who came to her office with friends one day, with questions about this aspect of her ministry. God gave him a personal demonstration:

"... as I took a step toward him and extended my hand to place on his shoulder to pray for him, his legs suddenly buckled . . . and he fell backwards to the floor . . . it was as though the whole room were filled with the glory of God. . . . His friends helped him to his feet and he started out the door, still shaking his head with a glow on his face that must have been like the glow that was on the face of Moses when he returned from Mt. Sinai. . . ."[23]

Charles and Frances Hunter in *Supernatural Horizons* speak of resting in the Spirit in Kathryn Kuhlman's meetings:

"After Charles and I were married, and we were traveling across the nation sharing the love of Jesus Christ, we heard some peculiar things about a woman named Kathryn Kuhlman. We heard that people had dramatic healings in her services and when they came forward to testify, she 'pushed them over!' This did not turn us off! Instead, it put a hungering in our hearts to see what this was that people were beginning to talk about. . . .

"We were in the Pittsburgh area . . . and discovered . . . that she was to be in the First Presbyterian Church. . . . (In the service) we watched things we had never seen before. We saw dramatic divine healings of all kinds. . . . When they came forward to testify of their healing, we noticed Kathryn Kuhlman just laid her hands on them and they all fell backwards. . . ."

Frances Hunter speaks of how Kathryn Kuhlman left the podium and began walking down the aisle. At one point Kathryn pointed directly at Frances and called her out into the aisle.

". . . She just laid those soft hands on my temples ever so gently and asked God to bless me, and bless me He did, because would you like to guess where I was? Right on the floor! And in my best dress besides, knowing I had to speak at a luncheon that day! I could have cared less. I felt as if I was in heaven. The Spirit of God had breathed on me and I felt like a feather as I went down! . . . My life has never been the same since that day when God's power went through my entire being.

". . . It was not long after I went under the power of God that Charles experienced this same supernatural touch from God. His life, like mine, has never been the same from the moment God personally touched him! Since that time God has let us see hundreds of thousands fall under the awesome power of the Spirit.

"Many have asked over the years, 'What good does it do?' When you have experienced this phenomenon, you will never be the same again because this is a divine touch upon your life placed there by the Almighty God! The transformed lives of individuals is the best testimony we know concerning this event."[24]

"Great are the works of the Lord; they are pondered by all who delight in them" (Psalm 111:2).

Testimonies

"It Happened in Rome . . ."
Father Arnulfo Shares His Story

Father Arnulfo Arandia is the former Director of the Charismatic Renewal in Ecuador. His first experience with resting in the Spirit occurred at the Charismatic Conference in Rome in 1984.

"I was ordained a priest in Ecuador in 1980, and for the first four years, my priesthood was a total and absolute waste. I used to celebrate Mass in 15 minutes, running. I yawned like every person in Mass. I was a weary priest.

"I made a trip to New York in 1984, dragging along with me all of my difficulties and disappointments. During that trip I had some plans about leaving the priesthood.

"I met a charismatic couple on that trip. They kept talking every day about the renewal. They talked about God when they got up, God for breakfast, God for lunch, God for supper, God here and God there. I would say to them in an insolent, arrogant way, 'Ah, talking about God! You have not studied theology, and you talk to me about God!'

(I studied theology for eight years.)

"They invited me to go to Rome with them. I said to myself, 'I'm going to have a good time and take advantage of the ticket they are giving to me.' I spent the whole week in Rome, during the talks, sleeping and snoring. It was a repetition of all I had studied in theology and philosophy. It was so boring. Then the moment of laying on of hands arrived, and I said to the lady, 'I didn't experience God.' She said, 'Arnulfo, try to be a little humble.'

"We were there in the place where the Pope and Cardinal Suenens were watching people being prayed over. Mother Teresa of Calcutta was also there. I was among all of them when a nun rested in the Spirit. I turned to look at her and started laughing. I said to the woman who had brought me there, 'Look at that nun. She fell like a dumpling.' The woman replied, 'Look, son, this is a sacred moment. They are laying on hands.' I turned to look and it was as if they had kicked me. Pum! I fell on the floor. Later I woke up, and it was like I had fainted. I didn't know what happened to me at that moment. I opened my eyes and saw a lot of old ladies crying. I said to myself, 'I died.' I looked up from the floor and asked the lady what happened to me. She said, 'This is the impact of God — resting in the Spirit.'

"Everything looked new after that. While I used to make long sermons, at that moment I felt the desire to avoid all that is related to science and methods. I said, 'From now on, the only method I am going to use for my homilies will be the word of God, and the only basic principles for my preaching will be the word of God and the experience of God.' "

"As I walked up the aisle at my first anointing service it seemed to take forever. I wanted my turn to come. I said, 'Lord, I want to feel Your presence. I want to know that You are real, that You are here. I need that to know and believe.' This was in 1981 at a healing service given by Father Robert DeGrandis. He taught on forgiveness, and my heart began to fill with love for all the people who had hurt me throughout my life. Then, when he spoke on resting in the Spirit,* I felt a growing excitement. I had traveled in fast circles, and was never satisfied. I had seen so many things that I thought, 'Nothing can surprise me now. I'm willing to see what Jesus has to offer.'

"Father DeGrandis told us that the Holy Spirit would touch us if we really wanted Him to do so. All we had to do was yield. He told us that the Holy Spirit was a gentleman and would never force Himself upon us. As I walked up the aisle I heard in my mind, 'He'll never do that for you, Matti. You aren't special enough. You have to be holy.' But I continued waiting in line. I was singing and praying as Father came closer. When I was anointed a cloud of white came over me and I fell into it. My first thought as I lay on the floor was, 'This is ridiculous. I did this on purpose because I wanted to go down.' But even as I said the words I knew it wasn't true. Jesus was there, ministering to me. My heart began to beat faster, and the blood in my veins grew warm, from my heart to the tips of my being. I said, 'Oh, Lord, please forgive me. I take it back. I know You are here.'

"I felt like I was on the floor for hours. I had such a wonderful, satisfying rest with Jesus. I knew I should

---

*Note that in the survey (see page 19), 62% of the individuals had received an explanation prior to the experience.

get up and make room for someone else. When I tried to get up I could hardly stand. I wobbled back to my seat while my mother-in-law sat watching me, grinning from ear to ear. She asked me later, 'Why did you get up so fast?' (I knew I had been on the floor at least 30 minutes.) She said, 'You were only on the floor three minutes.'

"I guess there are no time clocks in heaven!"

"When I Saw How Personal Jesus Was . . ."
Kari's Story

"My first deep experience of resting in the Spirit occurred at a conference of about 5,000 people in Southern California. At that time I had a number of physical problems stemming from an automobile accident two years previously, and was in constant pain. I had a cervical curvature in my neck, scoliosis, a pelvic tilt and one leg longer than the other.

"At first I wasn't sure I would be able to go to the conference, because the people I had planned to travel with were not sure they could go. I prayed with some friends, however, and was given a vision of a handkerchief. Along with that vision I received the scripture, 'God did extraordinary miracles through Paul, so that even handkerchiefs and aprons that had touched him were taken to the sick, and their diseases were cured . . .' (Acts 19:11-12). I knew I was to go.

"At the conference I went forward to receive prayer, realizing that the Lord had prepared a divine appointment. The team member told me later that she had been praying for the Lord to send 'just the right person' for her to pray for. She anointed me and prayed in detail for each physical condition, in what I describe as 'key point praying.' While I was resting in the Spirit I was totally healed of all of the physical problems.

"When I saw how personal Jesus was, and how intimately He cared about every detail of my life, I began to deepen my search. I had been baptized in the Spirit a month previously, when I was desperate and in great pain. This new encounter with His love created in me a desire for greater intimacy and greater discipline. This was the beginning of my real commitment to Jesus Christ."

AREN'T YOU GLAD WE ASKED? . . .
statistics continued

5. Are you aware of any healing when you rested in the Spirit the first time?

Yes	66%
No	31%
Not answered	3%

(There was a slightly higher percentage of women aware of healing. The figures show 63% of the men aware of healing compared with 68% of the women.)

The following indicates the percentages of the types of healing reported after their first experience of resting in the Spirit:

	Male*	Female*
Relationship	18%	15%
Physical	11%	13%
Mental	28%	30%
Spiritual	57%	48%

*Responses total more than 100% because respondents often checked more than one category.

6. Are you aware of any healing when you rested the THIRD time?

Yes	66%
No	19%
Not answered	15%

(Again, the women's figures are higher on awareness of healing, with 69% versus 60% of the men.)

The following indicates the types of healing reported after resting in the Spirit the THIRD time:

	Male*	Female*
Relationship	16%	20%
Physical	4%	12%
Mental	23%	28%
Spiritual	41%	45%

*Responses total more than 100% because respondents often checked more than one category.

. . . to be continued

Review of Key Points

* There are a number of references in scripture to people falling in the presence of God, voluntarily and involuntarily, for various reasons.

* Some saints in Catholic history tell of ecstatic states where physical strength vanishes and spiritual strength increases.

* The state of ecstasy seems to be similar to, but not identical with, the present-day experience of resting in the Spirit.

* Pentecostals around the world speak of conversions and empowering as individuals fall and are prostrated before the Lord.

* Hearing about dramatic healings can put a hunger in our hearts for more of God.

Prayer

Heavenly Father, please give me deep, biblical understanding of resting in the Spirit. I want to understand through Your word, and through personal experience.

Through resting in the Spirit, give me increased awareness of Your nature and goodness, as You did with the people in the *City of God*. Let their experience of joy and wonder be my experience also.

As with John Tauler, I want my inner and outer faculties conscious of a new strength; I want clear perception of unknown matters; I want teaching that comes directly from Your Spirit; I want a gift of understanding; I want to be a fit instrument of Your work.

As with the pentecostals, I want a yielded heart and purification from sin, pride and selfishness. Enable me, Father, to become a person of prayer.

Along with Father Arnulfo Arandia I want my work to be fruitful and powerful. Along with Mattie, I want a deep love for those who have hurt me. And along with Kari, I want greater intimacy with You and greater discipline in my personal life. Let this moment be for me the beginning of real commitment.

Heavenly Father, rest me in Your Spirit, and let the work begin. In Jesus' name. Amen.

"For the Lord is good and His love endures forever; His faithfulness continues through all generations" (Psalm 100:5).

3

He Leads Me Beside Quiet Waters

". . . He who has compassion on them will guide them and lead them beside springs of water" (Isaiah 49:10).

The purpose of this section is to provide a simple overview of how it looks and how it feels to rest in the Spirit — the external and internal view.

"All Those People Lying There . . ." The View From the Outside

Resting in the Spirit seems to be one of the ways God moves us into position, or sets up the dynamics, for us to receive healing. Father John Hampsch describes some of the healing methods through which resting in the Spirit can occur.

"Healing is ministered in several manners. It can be communicated by the laying on of hands by itself; by the stretching of one's hands out over a group; by the blessing of the sick with prayers from the ritual, or by benediction of the Blessed Sacrament. A whole group could lay hands on the shoulders and head of the person being prayed for, or several could be prayed for as a group, standing in a circle holding hands.

"The resting in the Spirit can happen within any of these contexts. Usually it happens with the laying on of hands, and/or anointing with blessed oil."[25]

The Setting:

"I was alone, taking my daily rest at a retreat. For 15-30 minutes I experienced such a strong presence of the Lord (electricity, vibrations, peace), that I felt I had to stay still. I thought I'd probably not even be able to move" (librarian).

"I often rest in the Spirit in small group meetings in a home. The Lord does deep inner healing in those times . . ." (wife and mother).

"Most of my experiences resting in the Spirit have been in large services of 200-1000 people, yet when I am on the floor I am alone with Jesus. He is speaking to me and loving me as if I am the only one in the room" (businesswoman).

The Position

"I was standing with a group praying for someone else to receive the baptism when I heard the leader say, 'Catch him, he's falling.' I thought he was talking about someone else, until I found myself on the floor . . ." (civil engineer).

"I have rested in the Spirit many times when already sitting . . ." (Benedictine nun).

"A friend prayed over me when I was laying down, and I rested deeply in the Spirit for 30 minutes" (teacher).

The Instrument

"Father DeGrandis asked me if I wanted to be baptized in the Holy Spirit. When I said 'Yes,' he touched me lightly and I fell to the floor" (data processing manager).

"There are times when it seems almost impossible to remain standing, even though nobody is touching or laying on hands" (homemaker).

Sensation While Falling

"I felt weightless, like an astronaut . . ." (clerk).

". . . like a leaf in the wind, drifting to the ground . . ." (mother).

"It felt like something heavy falling on me . . ." (data processing manager).

Change in Physical Senses While on the Floor

From the testimonies I have received, it seems that there is often a gentle, partial "anesthetizing" of the physical senses that enables a shift of focus from external to internal. As this shift occurs the spiritual world seems to come to life in a more powerful way.

Physical Expression

Peaceful, unpeaceful,* laughing, crying.

---

*Unpeaceful effects generally suggest the touching of deep emotional wounds or the replacing of negative influences with the presence of Jesus. See page 104.

Duration of Time on the Floor

The time can range from minutes to hours, depending probably upon the depth and extent of inner work being accomplished. "My experience has been of slight resting to resting for a long period. I have felt the Spirit come gently and swiftly, with different intensities" (secretary).

"I saw all those people lying there and I wondered what in the world God was doing . . ." (teacher).

"Caring, Holding, Rocking . . ." The View From the Inside

As mentioned in *The Healing Ministry,* the Lord often speaks to us at deep levels while resting in the Spirit:

"Many people have had the experience of having their life pass in front of them. . . . I believe when that happens in a prayerful situation, inner healing is taking place. . . ."[26]

The survey respondents shared a variety of ways in which the Lord touched their hearts. The following comments are representative of the feelings shared in the survey, and also reflect what I hear around the world, as I minister in leadership training workshops and healing services. They are grouped separately into male and female responses.

Men's Experiences

"It brings me closer to the Lord. It is a real lift to my spiritual growth" (retired journeyman machinist).
"When I rest in the Spirit I have an awesome aware-

ness of God's presence. I cannot relate to a particular time that I rested and received a distinct healing, yet over the years I have been healed of about six physical problems and several emotional problems. I have been praying for others for the past eight years and have seen many people rest in the Spirit" (business owner and permanent deacon).

"Resting in the Spirit has enabled me to trust God" (civil servant).

"It has helped bring my religion alive. I feel that I would never have reached my level of understanding without being able to rest in the Spirit. The Lord has a chance to work without interference from me"* (school administrator).

"It's a time of spiritual refreshment and provides a release from fear and anxiety" (district attorney investigator).

"It feels like falling in love. The peace and surrender are enormous. The memory lingers on as a spiritual assurance in dry times" (account clerk).

"The first time was at home alone.** I felt a definite presence of the Holy Spirit and it began a whole new relationship with the Lord" (teacher).

"I have seen people that have rested in the Spirit come to the Lord and back to the Church" (postal clerk).

"It is a total relaxation for me. Sometimes I am aware of what is going on around me, and sometimes I'm not. I feel totally at peace with my creator" (farm laborer).

"I rested in the Spirit at a retreat when we went to pray for the healing of our son. My first thoughts were

*See Question 12 on page 97. Ninety-four percent of the people feel resting in the Spirit has been a gift from God.

**See Question 10 on page 80. Fifty-four percent of the people in the survey have rested in the Spirit while alone.

negative, but at the time of resting in the Spirit I asked Jesus to help our son. I really began to feel the peace when I reached out and prayed for someone else who was resting in the Spirit'' (unidentified male).

"It was one of the most peaceful, loving, close-to-the-Lord times I have ever experienced" (salesman).

"My own experience of resting in the Spirit has been uneventful so far" (engineer).

"The first time I rested in the Spirit my oldest sister had just died. I was bitter and deeply grieved. My wife and I came forward for anointing. She had an arthritic hip. After she was rested, she got up healed. I got up with a vision of my sister walking hand in hand with Jesus" (truck driver).

"The first time changed my whole life. I started back to Mass, I became a better person and a better father to my kids" (inspector).

"Resting in the Spirit gives me that peaceful feeling that I have missed all my life" (data processing manager).

"It is an overwhelming feeling of God's love for me like a gentle caring, holding, rocking of a parent with a child" (administrator).

"... *blessed is the man who takes refuge in Him*" (Psalm 34:8).

Women's Experiences

"Fear had kept me from growing closer to the Lord. By resting in the Spirit I say to the Lord, 'Take me, I'm Yours. I want all that You want for me' " (registered nurse).

"I have been reluctant to rest in the Spirit when standing in a line, fearful about someone catching me when I fall" (nun).

"I have felt healed in body, mind and spirit — washed clean — renewed" (nun).

". . . I came away with excitement and the next morning all the songs I had always sung suddenly meant something" (homemaker).

"I am still sometimes uncomfortable with it" (office clerk).

"I have been able to look at myself in a different way, and realize that a contemplative approach to problems can be more rewarding than a critical one" (registered nurse).

"I wish I could feel more comfortable with it. If I am around people that are not charismatic I feel embarrassed. But after resting in the Spirit I feel so good I wish it could happen more often" (licensed practical nurse).

"I feel that I am just soaking in the Lord's love" (product designer).

"Sometimes I've wanted to yield to the Spirit and felt I have deliberately resisted" (court reporter).

"Each time I have felt the peace, the power and the presence of the Lord" (teacher).

"It improved my prayer life"* (housewife).

"I had a difficult time intellectually with resting in the Spirit, but within the last nine months I have become very teachable about this experience. I have a more intimate relationship with Jesus now and He helps me to understand the events of my life" (teacher).

"Some of the deepest healings I have received while resting in the Spirit are in relationship to my earthly father and my heavenly Father" (homemaker).

"I was surprised** the first time I rested in the Spirit

*See question 13 on page 97. Eighty-two percent of the people in the survey feel it has improved their prayer life.

**See question 4 on page 20. Sixty-nine percent of those surveyed were surprised.

because I thought it would be just for people who were more Spirit-filled than myself!'' (domestic worker).

"The first time I rested in the Spirit I was healed of arthritis in my legs, back and hands, which I had had for several years. I feel that the major gift received while resting in the Spirit is a renewed, closer relationship with the Lord'' (retired school principal).

"At first I didn't like the idea of laying on the floor with other people around. Now the Lord has taken that away and has replaced it with a deep loving peace each time I rest'' (cook).

"I have been very touched by seeing my children rest in the Spirit. They respond with such simple faith and their reaction is always one of joy'' (homemaker).

"I feel like I'm being loved by God'' (nurse's aide).

"I received the gift of so much love that I could hardly stand it'' (cafeteria manager).

"When I was new in the renewal I was tremendously insecure and could not believe I was loved. The first time I rested in the Spirit, I encountered the love of Jesus'' (housewife).

"About ten years ago after prayer and resting in the Spirit I was healed of four dislocated discs''* (librarian).

"I think it is a total introduction to God's glory prior to getting to heaven!'' (manicurist).

". . . We have seen His glory, the glory of the one and only Son, who came from the Father, full of grace and truth'' (John 1:14).

---

*See question 11 on page 80. Fifty-four percent of the people in the survey report major healing while resting in the Spirit.

Testimonies

"I Remember What Mom Had Said . . ." Vince's Story

"Ruth had told me about resting in the Spirit, but I was determined not to go down. First of all, I was wearing my best suit and I didn't want it to get dirty on the gymnasium floor. Second, I thought it was a sign of weakness for the supervisor of the department of social services with all of that status, to lay on the floor. Third, I remembered what Mom had said about the 'crazy alleluias.' In 1936 we lived in front of a Baptist church where people called each other 'brother' and 'sister,' prayed in tongues and fell on the floor. Mom used to say, 'See, those are the "crazy alleluias." Never get tangled up with that group.' So there we were, doing those very things at a Catholic prayer meeting, many years later. The fourth reason I was determined not to go down was that I considered myself a macho. I figured the only one that could knock me down would be another macho. But the Holy Spirit is a super-macho. He doesn't care how big we are. He doesn't care about our status. He'll knock us down if we will just open the door a little. He has the power. I found myself on the floor. I didn't care about macho. I was in the arms of Jesus Christ and He was touching me and ministering to me and loving me. All of the hate and anger and bitterness in my heart just died away. I was transformed, created into a new person. The old Vincent stayed on the floor, and the new Vincent got up with Jesus Christ. I stopped drinking. I stopped smoking. I stopped being worldly. I came back to the Catholic Church. . . ."*

---

*See question 5 on page 39. Fifty-seven percent of the men received spiritual healing when they first rested in the Spirit.

". . . I sing in the shadow of Your wings. I stay close to You; Your right hand upholds me" (Psalm 63:7-8).

"A Touch of Goodness . . ." Irene's Story

"I saw the people 'falling in the Spirit' at the healing service and was awed by it. What did actually happen to make them do this? I didn't think too much about it because I was busy enjoying singing the hymns while we waited, and reassuring my friend Barbie that she would be okay and that I would not fall. As we stood in front of the railing, I began to pray, focused in on the crucifix above the altar and praying for the Holy Spirit to let His light enter my heart, my mind and my soul. I said, 'I give myself to You completely. Do with me as You will.' I kept saying this and then sensed Father Matthew coming nearer. There was a feeling of some special excitement. I watched Barbie in case she needed my help. Then Father Matthew placed one hand on my head and one hand on my shoulder. I started saying a prayer about Light, and felt myself being pulled backward, losing control. I grabbed the priest's hand to steady myself. I couldn't feel my body, as if it weren't there.

"When I got up from the floor and returned to my seat I missed the kneeler and started to fall sideways. My legs were so weak they couldn't hold me up. I burst into tears, sobbed my love to the Lord and just kept saying, 'Thank You for touching me.' I sat down, feeling warm and still weak. I had the sensation of trembling inside my body and I thought surely my hands were shaking, but when I looked down they were quietly resting in my lap. People were talking around me, but I didn't want to join in. I just wanted to sit there and savor the feeling.

"On the way home I felt sort of drained, like I didn't want to speak. When I did speak, it was slowly. After a while at home I talked with my husband, Willis. I wanted to share my feelings with him. It was as if there was a goodness in and around me that I wanted to share. Going to bed we talked again.

"I knew why God had to touch us through our feelings. There are no words in our language to describe it, so we can't truly communicate with words. That's why there are so many mysteries; things we can't understand. God's 'language' is so far above us. That is why we say we will understand all in heaven in the presence of the Holy Trinity. Then we will all speak the same language.

"I had a description of the way I felt — 'peaceful excitement.' It was not nervous and jittery excitement that would keep me awake, but peaceful acceptance of God's gift . . . being excited with the gift I had just received. Before I fell asleep, I had the same feeling I had at Notre Dame when I felt the presence of the Lord so strongly when I sat before the Blessed Sacrament.

"It was okay with me if I died that night, because I was in a state of grace. But I thought of my family and said, 'Maybe I'd better stay awhile; just stay close to me, Lord.' Later, when I got up in the middle of the night, I was aware that through my mind was going the song, 'Just as I Am.' I smiled because apparently I had been singing and praying while I slept. Praise God!

"This good feeling remained all through the next day. I felt there was something special about me — not me, but God-in-me. I thought I must be radiating His love and goodness and that everyone would notice that I was different. Apparently, outwardly I didn't look different. I just felt new. Nothing could shake my peace that day. I looked forward to going to church that evening . . . not looking for any great miracle, but just to be there. I thanked God as soon as I got to the pew for allowing me to be there. The priest affirmed my feelings. Unworthy as I am, it really did happen. He touched me!''

"Me? You Care About Me?" Evelyn's Story

"Before I rested in the Spirit I had many questions and concerns. The Lord provided me with a friend, a nun, who patiently answered these questions. Because of her patience, before I went to my first healing service my mind was prepared for the experience.* She explained that I would be anointed with oil on my forehead and that I would probably feel weightless and relaxed. She said that if I fell backwards there would be a catcher, so I wouldn't have to worry about getting hurt. And, she said that if I didn't rest in the Spirit, there was nothing wrong with me. When the anointing time came, I was mentally prepared. The priest made the sign of the cross with oil on my forehead, saying, '(You) were marked as belonging to Christ by the Holy Spirit . . .' (Ephesians 1:13). I felt myself lightly, weightlessly, falling backwards into the arms of my husband, who gently laid me on the floor.

"My mind was ready for the experience, but my heart was not prepared for the overwhelming feeling of God's presence and love. I heard Him say, 'Evelyn, you have been so concerned about the needs of others. Now just relax, it's your turn. Let me show you how much I love and care for you.' I felt like a baby cradled in its mother's arms, receiving undivided attention. I felt Christ pour out His loving attention and care on me. He permeated to the very depths of my heart. A sense of surprise at all the attention made me ask, 'Me? You care about me!' ''

*Note in question 1 on page 19 that 62% of the people in the survey were similarly mentally prepared.

"Cast all your anxiety on Him because He cares for you" (1 Peter 5:7).

AREN'T YOU GLAD WE ASKED? . . .
statistics continued

7. Did you seek to rest in the Spirit the first time?

Yes	48%
No	50%
Not answered	2%

   (The figures indicate that 55% of the men sought the initial experience, compared with 45% of the women.)

8. Did you seek to rest in the Spirit the THIRD time?

Yes	63%
No	25%
Not answered	12%

   (On the THIRD occasion, 68% of the men sought the experience, compared with 61% of the women.)

   . . . to be continued

Review of Key Points

* Resting in the Spirit can occur while alone, in small groups and in large groups.

* Resting can occur while standing, sitting or lying down.

* Resting can occur with or without an intermediary.

* A sense of weightlessness often accompanies the fall.

* Resting is often accompanied by a shift of focus from the external to the internal world.

* The time on the floor can vary from seconds to an hour or more.

* The experience varies from slight sense of peace to deep healing and transformation.

* Almost everyone senses God's loving presence in some way.

Prayer

Heavenly Father, I want to know You in ways I have never known You before. With the men in the survey, I want a deeper awareness of Your presence, refreshment and release from anxieties, closer union with You and knowledge of Your overwhelming love.

With the women in the survey, I want to feel washed clean, excited, intimacy with You, deep healing, peace and awareness of Your power.

With Vince, I want to lose my worldliness; with Irene, I want to truly learn Your language; with Evelyn, I want to receive Your undivided attention.

Thank You, Heavenly Father, for the wonderful ways You are working in my life. Make me an instrument of healing for others. In Jesus' name. Amen.

"For great is Your love, higher than the heavens; Your faithfulness reaches to the skies" (Psalm 108:4).

4

He Restores My Soul

"And the God of all grace, who called you to His eternal glory in Christ, after you have suffered a little while, will Himself restore you and make you strong, firm and steadfast" (I Peter 5:10).

Testimonies and Reflections of Priests and Nuns

In this section priests and nuns will share about resting in the Spirit, primarily as communicators of the gift.

"You May Be Right, But . . ."
Father Jack Reports From Australia

Father Jack Soulsby from Queensland reflects on his experiences:
"I first heard of this phenomenon early in 1975 when I was studying at Nemi, outside of Rome. Some folks had witnessed resting in the Spirit at a prayer group and related their experiences, doubts and fears to me. There had been no explanations, which led to some hesitations about the experience. This situation illustrated to me the need for good teaching.
"On a charismatic retreat for priests in Sydney in 1987

Father DeGrandis gave our group teaching on resting in the Spirit. The results were phenomenal. What remained with me, especially, was the recognition that we need to not only be open to the experience, but to desire it. On evaluation of the retreat, the majority of the priests said they experienced peace. I personally experienced Our Lady present, and saying to me: 'You give me much joy, for you seek to do the will of my Son.' Ten months later that experience was just as vivid and life-giving.

"On occasions where people have rested in the Spirit in my ministry I have had people come up and say, 'I don't believe all of this is of God.' I often respond by saying, 'Would you stand there for a moment?' Then I will call out to a few who have been resting, 'Peter, would you tell my friend here what that experience was like?' He would say, 'Oh, such peace!' Then I would say, 'John, would you tell my friend about your experience?' 'I saw Jesus. . . .' " After about four or five testimonies I would turn to my critic and say, 'Now, you may be right that all this is not from God, but into your theory you now have to fit what you've just heard!' "

"Focus on Change . . ." Report From a Minnesota Priest

Father Robert Voigt from Holdingford reflects on the experience:

"The phenomenon of resting in the Spirit came to St. Cloud, Minnesota, around 1980 when Father Luke Zimmer of California preached a mission at Gilman. After the Eucharist he blessed people with a relic of the True Cross, and they crumbled one after the other. I observed this, marveled at it, studied it and became eager to have the experience myself. One evening I went out to Gilman, prayed for the experience and was blessed by Father

Luke. Nothing happened externally or in my heart as far as I knew. I was disappointed.

"A year later Father Luke gave a mission in my parish, Holy Angels, in St. Cloud. Again he blessed all the people after Mass with his relic. He started by blessing the priests in the sanctuary. Father Mark went down with a resounding crack. Father Luke came up to me. Before he ever touched me, I fell. It was sudden, and fast, and unplanned. I was somewhat embarrassed in the presence of my congregation, yet it was restful. I felt like staying there a long time. When I arose, I was grateful for the experience. The phenomenon has occurred on several occasions since that time. Often when I bless people and they are overcome by the Spirit, they tell me they receive a healing.

"I have come to see that the Holy Spirit can work more easily for a person's betterment at this time. Just as the Holy Spirit can work effectively on a person in a dream when the mind is relaxed, He can work well when the body is relaxed. As one author put it, 'When God does surgery, the floor is His operating table.'

"I personally find a great comfort in the presence of this phenomenon in our Church. At a time when the faith is very weak, we need extra gifts such as this one. I do not readily pray for resting in the Spirit in a large, unbelieving crowd, but in a charismatic group or with an individual, I will ask the Lord for the gift to be manifested. At the same time I remind myself that the emphasis should not be on this gift as much as on what happens inside. The increase of faith, the growth of divine love, the healing of the body and spirit — these are the great values. While not denigrating the sign, I focus upon the change of heart."

"They Call Her 'Sister Alleluia' . . ."
A Nun From Puerto Rico Shares Her Story

Sister Carmen Parilla is a Montessori preschool teacher in Menlo Park, California, active with Spanish prayer group leadership, jail and hospital ministries and healing teams. As the only charismatic nun in her order, she has been nicknamed "Sister Alleluia" by others in her convent. She shares here some experiences of resting in the Spirit.

"I had been going to prayer groups for about six months when some friends drove me to a meeting with a lay evangelist at a Catholic church in San Francisco. It was a healing service, and when people went to him for prayer, they would fall down on the floor. No one had ever told me about this phenomenon, and I thought he was pushing them over. I said to myself, 'I'm not going up there!'

"Someone in the group shared a vision in which an angel of the Lord came down and spread oil on the people. I could see oil on some of the Bibles, and knew something powerful was happening.

"A person asked me to go up for prayer. I held back at first, then finally decided to go forward. The evangelist put three fingers very lightly on my forehead and simply said, 'You are healed.' I went down. A man put a blanket over me and left me alone on the floor.

"When I was on the floor I had a vision of people standing around dressed in white. I saw angels coming down and blessing the people. All the time I knew that I was awake, but I couldn't seem to get up.

"The church was almost empty when a man came over and helped me get up. 'How do you feel?' he asked. 'I'm okay,' I replied. 'It's time to go. You had a long rest.

God bless you.'

"It was the most beautiful experience I ever had. I felt wonderful! From that time on I was more sure of the love the Lord had for me. I knew that He really cared for me.

"Soon after that experience I went through a Spanish life in the Spirit seminar and began praying over people. They would feel a heat coming through my hands and into their bodies. They too would then rest in the Spirit as I had done.

"Sometimes people would say, 'Pray for me, but I don't want to fall down.' I would say, 'It's important that you don't resist the Holy Spirit. But if you just release yourself into the hands of the Lord so that His power can work, that is the important thing. You don't have to rest in the Spirit to be healed, but just be open to receive healing. In my experience, most people who go down will be healed in some way, because they have released themselves and opened themselves to His healing power. Sometimes people keep sins in themselves and won't forgive, and that makes it hard for God to set them free. When they let go and let Him work, something causes them to want to do right for other people.

"One time a woman came to me and said the doctor told her she could never have children. When I prayed for her to be able to conceive, she rested in the Spirit. The following year when I was at the Vallombrosa Retreat Center in Menlo Park, a woman came up to me holding a beautiful blue-eyed girl. She asked, 'Are you Sister Carmen?' When I said, 'Yes,' she told me that she was the one I had prayed for to be able to conceive. She had become pregnant shortly after I prayed for her.

"I have heard many wonderful reports of deliverance from witchcraft, drugs and spirit-possession as people have rested in the Spirit in my ministry. (But mostly it is spiritual and emotional healing.) I don't know how God does it; there is no explanation for what He does. But I like being 'Sister Alleluia,' and seeing God work in such wonderful ways.''

"God in His Goodness . . ." Reflections and Testimonies From the Ministry of Father Ralph DiOrio

Father Ralph DiOrio, in *A Miracle to Proclaim,* reflects upon mankind's universal hunger to be touched by a living God:

". . . people come (to healing services) because of the healing virtue, the healing power of the Holy Spirit dwelling among the contemporary disciples. And no matter how large or how small the assembly gathered together may be, the fact remains that God is alive, and the children of God are dependent on this power.

"When human lives gather together in the atmosphere of the Holy Spirit, God touches those lives positively. These people will receive God's goodness for them. In every human person some form of faith resides. That faith may be stifled, dusty with years of unuse, perplexed or hazy, perhaps even deliberately turned off. But it is there! All it awaits is the moment of being hopefully activated through some form of affirmation. People are the same everywhere. They all have the same hunger and the same response to either personal or en masse evangelism. They yearn for some 'Good News.' "

The following testimonies of healing during resting in the Spirit are reported by Father DiOrio in this book:

* A seventeen-year-old youngster with cancer of the knee bone: ". . . As Dan stood up and put his crutches under his arms for support, Father came

right over and brought him into the center aisle. . . . As Father prayed, my son fell backward, slain in the Spirit. . . . Afterward Dan said that he felt a warm sensation pass through his leg." (Dan was healed.)

* Boy with an inoperable brain tumor: "While everyone was praying (at a healing service in Massachusetts) '. . . I put my arm around my son and began to place this cross that had been blessed by father on Chris's head. As I asked Jesus to please cure him, the cross flew out of my hand and appeared to weld itself to my son's head . . . he went flying backward . . . slain in the Spirit. When my son awakened, he said that the pain in his head was excruciating. This was unusual, as he did not have any pain prior to being slain in the Spirit. 'It feels like the middle of my head blew up,' he told us. The center of his head was the exact location of his tumor. . . . His brain tumor not only stopped growing, but entirely disappeared. . . .' "

* A nun with an injured shoulder and a need for inner healing. While resting in the Spirit at a healing service, she had a deep experience with the Lord. ". . . When I came to, Father Ralph was gone. But God in His goodness had seen to it that Father Mike was nearby. Just as the Good Shepherd held His lost sheep, he held me gently as I cried and cried. That night I received inner healing as God relieved me of the hurts that were in my heart." The following morning at Father Ralph's private Mass, he prayed for her again, and she rested again. "When I got up I was radiant and my shoulder was healed. In His everlasting love, He healed my shoulder. But even more important, He healed my unbelief!"[27]

"Praise the Lord, O my soul; all my inmost being, praise His holy name" (Psalm 103:1).

"The Proof Was in the Experience . . ."
An Irish Skeptic Tells His Story

Father John Kenny, SS.CC., of Oakland, California, shares his experiences:

"The first time I experienced the phenomenon of resting in the Spirit was at a community retreat. Part of the retreat entailed prayer of healing for members of the community who wanted to avail themselves of the experience. As I watched from the back of the church a number of our men went forward to be prayed over. I was stuck to my seat with no intention of going forth. My intention was strengthened when I saw one of the brothers fall backward and lie on the floor. I remember thinking that he must have been pushed. If I had known this would happen on another retreat, I never would have gone.

"The next time it happened was on a retreat given by Father DeGrandis. During that retreat he gave a brief explanation of resting in the Spirit and then invited us to experience the power of the Holy Spirit by yielding to this charism. He gave a few non-conclusive scripture passages, such as that of St. Paul falling to the ground. I didn't pay much attention to the teaching, because I had no intention of going down flat on my back. I felt stuck and obligated, however, when the rest of the priests were prayed over. I went forward expecting nothing, or that maybe he would give me a push and catch me off balance and I would fall. The one good thing I noticed was that he placed a man behind me to catch me if I fell backward. As he went down the line I noticed a number of the others going down. I thought they were probably just susceptible to the power of suggestion. They wanted it so badly that they were faking it. When my turn came I was nervous, both about going down and not going down. If I didn't go down would it mean I had some defect? Father De-Grandis came to me and began to pray over me by having his right hand a few inches from my forehead. To this day I am not sure exactly what happened. I felt myself falling backwards, almost floating, and he had not so much as laid a finger on me. I rested on the floor for a few minutes, fully conscious of all that was happening around me and very much at peace.

"Since then I have rested in the Spirit a number of times, and have always received healing. Frequently when I pray for people they will also rest in the Spirit. I rejoice in the power of the Holy Spirit at work. For me, the proof was in experiencing the experience."

It is interesting that most priests have a negative attitude toward resting in the Spirit until they experience it themselves. Perhaps this is because their whole approach to God has been more intellectual than experiential. Many priests have said to me that they never learned to pray in the seminary. Father Karl Rahner, S.J., the famous German theologian, has said that the Christian of the future will be a mystic, or he will not be anything. This seems to mean that Christians will be people of deep religious experience. The Church of the future will be a Church of deep religious experience. Resting in the Spirit will probably be a part of this life-style.

"Every Knee Shall Bow . . ." Stories From
the Ministry of Father Rick Thomas in El Paso

In El Paso, Texas, on the Mexican border, the ministry of Father Rick Thomas is legendary. Rene Laurentin, a well-known theologian, tells his story in *Miracles in El Paso?* Two testimonies are shared below:

"Sometime in 1978, the director of the city prison of Juarez, Jesus Galindo Fernandez, came to Our Lady's Youth Center to ask for Rick Thomas' help.

" 'These people are without hope; they are incorrigible,' he said. 'Only the power of God can change them. We'd like to have you come and help us in any way you can.'

"To prepare themselves for this new ministry, the community made a retreat from August 17 to 19, 1979, at the Lord's Ranch.

" 'The first visit was unspeakable,' writes Rick Thomas. 'The stench of urine filled the place. Prisoners were yelling, jeering at us, cursing. Even with the loudspeaker we had brought, our voices could not be heard in the uproar.'

"Confident that the Lord could do the impossible, the musicians that had come with us began to play a song based on Philippians 2:10-11: 'Jesus is His name. Every knee shall bow, every tongue confess that Jesus Christ is Lord.'

"After an hour and a half these words came true. A number of inmates were on their knees weeping. Several sank to the hard cement floor of the prison. The tension at the beginning had given way to total relaxation, a sort of calm and peaceful swoon. Some experienced what is sometimes referred to in charismatic circles as 'resting in the Spirit.'

" 'In this new atmosphere the guards, at first on the defensive, opened one cell to the visitors. Prisoners began to flock to us, asking us to pray over them, for them, and with them. About thirty-five thronged around us, and many felt a deep experience of the Lord.'

"The warden was dumbfounded and remarked that the first to come forward were the most incorrigible of the prisoners."

"Therefore God exalted him to the highest place and gave him the name that is above every name, that at the name of Jesus every knee should bow, in heaven and on earth and under the earth, and every tongue confess that Jesus Christ is Lord . . ."
(Philippians 2:9-11).

Father Rick Thomas also tells of a venture in the Lord among young delinquents.

"On February 9, 1981, the director of the Escuela de Mejoramiento Social para Menores (School of Social Rehabilitation for Minors) approached us with a request for our help. We accepted. It is 'home' for young Mexican detainees, a stone's throw from the Rio Grande along the Mexican-Texas border. We go every Monday morning. We begin with prayer outside before entering the white building. Then we ring the bell and the action begins. There are about seventy boys and some girls, seven at last count. We divide them into three groups, according to the three sections in which these children are kept. We proceed as in prison, with some adaptations.

"First we get the children to sing hymns and praise God. Then we tell them that God loves them and wants to help them change their life. After that we take them individually, those who want to, and teach them to pray. They ask God to change their heart, and every week we see deep experiences with the Lord. This is the bright side of our ministry.

"Every Monday, 80% of the young detainees in the white building yield to prayer. It is an impressive sight, these tense and exasperated children resting in the Spirit. They lie flat on the cement floor, sometimes for an hour or longer. And when they get up, they are different, filled with hope and peace. After this inner healing their witness is infectious. Doctor R.P. Lopez, the Director of the School of Social Rehabilitation, is delighted with the results and cooperates with us. The atmosphere of the 'home' has changed.

"The Director has asked us to come every day, not every week. But where can we find the time? We haven't found it yet."[28]

"*. . . He will quiet you with His love . . .*" (Zephaniah 3:17).

"My Perception of Resting in the Spirit . . ."
Report From a Cautious California Bishop

Bishop Donald Montrose of Stockton, California, has been involved with the charismatic renewal since 1978. In the parish where he was once a pastor, there was a rather large weekly prayer meeting. The following comments are based upon his observations as a regular participant in that meeting.

"I do not think resting in the Spirit is beneficial for a large prayer group. There are so many people that are wondering what is happening and it raises such questions in the mind of those who are new or who have recently arrived, that I think the effect is very divisive. It was for this reason that I tried to avoid resting in the Spirit as much as possible. When the prayer group was over and

68

when the regular time for prayer and Mass was over, there was always individual prayer. I used to ask the people requesting individual prayer to kneel at the communion rail or sit in a pew or a chair. This minimized resting in the Spirit. However, even in these circumstances there were people who rested in the Spirit.

"For this reason I believe that it is an authentic experience. If the Lord wishes someone to rest in the Spirit, there is nothing anyone can do regardless of what precautions might have been taken. What happens when people rest in the Spirit is not always apparent. In general, I believe that there is some interior healing that takes place and people usually are much more peaceful when they wake up.

"There are also some negative things that happen occasionally when people rest in the Spirit. . . . I am not sure about the cause of these manifestations.* However, I do think that when people rest in the Spirit they are in a defenseless position spiritually and perhaps if there is some predisposition in some way that negative spiritual influences become manifest. This is another reason why I do not think resting in the Spirit is generally beneficial in a large prayer group."

"It Must Be Their Sugar Levels . . ."
Father Tom Reports From New York

Father Tom McCormick from Medford, New York, shares some thoughts and experiences:
"The first time I heard the term 'slain in the Spirit,' was during the spring of 1974. Having been baptized in the Holy Spirit only a few years, and coming back from

---

*See page 104 for further comment on the "negative" things which can occur while resting in the Spirit.

my four years in the Air Force, I was finishing the second semester of my first year at one of the local colleges here in New York. A number of us decided to take a ride to Notre Dame for the conference of 1974. During that drive one of the girls in the group shared her experience of being 'slain in the Spirit' at a local fundamentalist church. My first reaction was one of question and dismay. 'Slain in the Spirit? What does that mean?'

"She told me that there was a time in part of the service in which the people were just 'overcome by the Holy Ghost,' as the preacher would call it. Again my reaction was one of question and concern. The more this woman shared about being 'slain in the Spirit,' the more confused we became. She told us of how people fell on the floor, and how they were being caught by others. It was hard to understand. Initially, I suspected that 'it must be something unique to the protestant churches.' How wrong I was!

"The first time I witnessed someone slain in the Spirit was in Atlantic City at a conference in 1977. It was a very clear, sunny afternoon. There were people praising the Lord on the boardwalk. My good friend Richie and I decided to take a walk and just enjoy God's presence. It was not unusual to see small groups of people singing and praising and praying with one another. However, my eyes caught sight of one particular group praying over a woman. As they prayed over her, I saw her fall back and hit the boardwalk. My first instinct was to run over and help her. My friend Richie pulled me back and told me that she was overcome by the power of the Holy Spirit. He explained to me what happened. It was then that I was able to understand that the Lord Jesus Christ was oftentimes really moving in great power in the individuals who were experiencing this phenomenon.

"I found over the years, even before I was ordained a priest, that God in fact does seem to work in this particular way in prayer group settings. I can recall instances of praying with a team of people and feeling a great surge of power as our group prayed. As a priest I have experienced the Lord moving in great power on thousands of occasions.

"I also have experienced great criticism from brother priests and some of our Catholic intellectuals who found it all too difficult to accept the fact that something was happening to these particular individuals. Such statements as 'It's all emotionalism,' 'It's fake,' 'It must be their sugar levels,' seemed to be common statements as I moved and prayed with people over the years. Personally I do believe that our Lord Jesus does work and move in people who are resting with Him. I have seen people resting for as long as an hour or as short as a few minutes. I have seen people's facial expressions change as God moved and worked within them.

"I also have experienced people resting in the Spirit in the confessional, as they shed their sins and ask God's forgiveness. The simple prayers of the Church have profoundly touched them and they have just quietly rested in the chair. Praying with people over the telephone and have them rest with the Lord is something that has happened also. But the caution that I would give to anyone who is reading this, is first that it is not you or I, for we are all sinners who need to be ministered to and healed by the Lord. But if God chooses to use a particular situation, whether it is in a counselling office or a confessional or on a telephone or at a eucharistic service, then God will choose to do that.

"I'm sure that I could give many other examples of experiences that I have had over the years with people.

I would say very simply that I believe that God does work in this area. I believe that people need to be pastored and taught, however.

"My primary concern is that some people look for the experience. They seem to look for the high. They look for the need to fall down, and to have the feeling while not holding onto the truth and the faith and the steadfastness that would come along with a life-relationship with Jesus Christ.

"Many people, too, look at a priest or a team who might be praying with someone, and say, 'Let's go over there. They've got the power.' Or, 'Let's go see how many people he can knock down.' The difficulty that I see in this regard would be stemming the tide of need and emotionalism associated with the phenomenon of resting in the Spirit. For example, many people are attracted to healing services, but few people seem to be willing to accept the fidelity of going, for example, to a weekly prayer meeting. Many people come to healing services or Masses to look and to see, to wait and to watch, before they come up to find out what it is all about. I've heard people say to me, 'Well, the only reason I came here was because my cousin told me that people fall down. I found that hard to believe, so I came to see for myself.'

"I believe that we need to focus on the giver of the gift, and not on the one who is praying with and over the people. I believe that the Lord is once again pointing out to us that we need to be dependent upon Him as our personal Lord and Savior.

"My prayer would be the same prayer as always, that we come to experience the life, the breath and the gift of Jesus Christ as Lord. That we come to see Him in all that we do. That we look to the power of the cross and not to the high feeling of the moment. My prayer is that we come to realize that Jesus Christ does work in the most simple and ordinary moments.

"I can remember the caution and concern about resting in the Spirit expressed by Father George Maloney in *Crux of the News* magazine around 1980. I would concur and offer my concern, and my warning. If people are going to healing Masses and services just for the natural high, then I would ask them to please re-evaluate their reasoning. Let the Lord be the Lord: Let the Lord work in the hearts of His people. God is going to do it. No priest, no religious, no lay person does it — it is the Lord. We all are being invited to pray with each other and for each other, and I would just finally add that it is my prayer that we seek the mystery, we seek the truth, and we ask our Mother Mary to be our intercessor."

"Falling Isn't Resting . . ."
Father Jim From Scotland Issues a Caution

In a letter to the editor of this book, Father Jim McManus, a Redemptorist theologian/author from Scotland, reflects on the approach of this author on the use of the charismatic gifts, and the phenomenon of resting in the Spirit:

". . . (Father DeGrandis) is the only teacher I know in the charismatic renewal who describes the charism, tells how to receive it and how to use it. He teaches how to make oneself available, humanly, for the gift and the operation of the gift. This, of course, presumes great faith. We ask God for the gift and then we use it. Most people, I feel, ask God for the gifts and then wait for God to tell them that they have received them. That really is not faith. Faith is when we act on 'ask and you shall receive.' His (Father DeGrandis') gift is to convince people that this is how gifts are given and how they function. We ask for them and then we use them.

"Resting in the Spirit has always been problematic for me. The very phrase itself, 'resting in the Spirit,' assumes that what happens is the work of the Spirit. Two people come forward for prayer. One falls backwards and the other remains standing. If the former is said to be 'resting in the Spirit' should we not logically say that the latter is 'standing in the Spirit'?

"I prefer to approach this question descriptively. We describe what happens. People fall down backwards. (That in itself is puzzling.) As John Richards, an Anglican theologian put it, 'We are dealing with the falling down phenomenon!' Now we must discern what is happening. People usually say that they experience great peace, prayerfulness and closeness to God. (I have experienced that myself.) Such prayerfulness is surely a gift of the Spirit and when one is experiencing this new sense of closeness to God, while lying on one's back, one can surely say that the person is resting in the Spirit.

"My problem is with equating the physical phenomenon of falling with the action of the Spirit. Each phenomenon in the spiritual life, whether it be tongues or prophecy or falling down is fundamentally ambiguous. It has to be discerned. It could be from the Holy Spirit, it could be from the subconscious, or it could be from the evil spirit. As Ann and Barry Ulanov write in *Religion and the Unconscious*:

> 'We recognize that the "unconscious" as a term leaves much to be desired, but there is no better one at present, and much of what the world of religion consigns to the spirit is clearly to be found in what depth psychology calls the unconscious.'[29]

"I see nothing wrong with applying the term 'resting in the Spirit' to a person who is actually lying on his back, intensely aware of God's love and presence. That person is resting in the Lord. But to apply the term to the actual physical phenomenon is to pre-judge the question. Falling down is not resting. To fall one has to yield and surrender and this act of yielding and surrendering can come either from the gift of grace or from the subconscious. Because it can come from the subconscious I personally try not to minister in such a way as to facilitate it. In other words, I don't encourage people to seek prayer standing up with their hands raised.

"I have heard people giving biblical examples of 'resting in the Spirit.' I must say that I find such explanations very forced. I don't think there is a single biblical case of what people in the renewal today call 'resting in the Spirit.'

"Having said all that, I want to repeat that when I have fallen down and lay on my back I experienced great peacefulness and prayerfulness."

[I would respond to Father Jim McManus in this fashion: Nature gives us a fear of falling backward; therefore, if one does fall backward while focused on Jesus Christ, this is probably the work of the Holy Spirit. The deeply positive spiritual effects support the conclusion that this is the work of the Holy Spirit. Our statistics also support this position.]

"Would You Like to Stop Sucking Your Thumb? . . ."
Sister Francis Clare's Personal Reflections
and Challenging Stories

"When I was travelling to a service with Charles and Frances Hunter one time, I said, 'If there is one thing that I would be afraid of in my healing ministry, it would be if God ever used me to rest people in the Spirit. I don't think that is very Catholic.' When I began to pray with them at that service for God to touch 'whatever and whoever,' I saw God's miraculous power poured out. Many people rested in the power of the Spirit. I secretly wondered if it would happen without the Hunters. Later, when I prayed with college prayer groups in Minnesota, I saw the same thing. I began to see and understand that it had nothing to do with human personalities. . . ."

"*. . . fan into flame the gift of God, which is in you . . .*" (2 Timothy 1:6).

Sister Francis Clare comments about the value of resting in the Spirit in the spiritual direction setting:

"We need to be very sensitive to our own limitations and open to God's desiring to move in a sovereign way. When I start to pray I begin in my natural mind, but when I feel Jesus saying, 'Let me take over,' I tell the person, 'I think Jesus would like to take over from here, and I'm going to just ask Him to rest you in the Spirit so He can give you the vision and He can give you the word, and He can give you the sense of direction.' In doing that, I am 'letting go and letting God.' I often witness that He will do in two seconds what would take me two hours, two days, two weeks, two months, or two years to accomplish.

"When people are resting they seem to be in a state of heightened spiritual awareness, in a place to speak to God and hear from God. Sometimes they see things they can't when they aren't under the power of God. So I encourage people to really rest, even if it seems like nothing is happening. Maybe just a little thought will come. I encourage

76

them to dialogue with that thought. 'God, is that what You are doing?' Then listen. Or, God may show them a little bit of something, and they respond, 'God, what is the meaning of that?'

"I pray for God to just sovereignly open them to what He is doing and what He wants to do. I encourage them to move with the direction He gives. They have many breakthroughs as they allow the Holy Spirit to lead them from grace to grace and glory to glory."

"And we, who with unveiled faces all reflect the Lord's glory, are being transformed into His likeness with ever increasing glory, which comes from the Lord, who is the Spirit" (2 Corinthians 3:18).

She shares about an experience in Germany:

"I was called to minister with a conference of 1200 youth, giving a main address entitled 'Would You Give God Permission to Meet You Where You're At?' As I gave the talk with the translator, the group responded by standing and saying, 'God I give You permission to meet me where I'm at.' They were in many different places. Some knew that people know that God exists, but they themselves had never experienced Him. Others knew a set of truths in their heads; others had some kind of personal experience with Jesus. Some had known the fullness of the Holy Spirit. They were in many different places.

"After the address, an invitation was made for further ministry upstairs. The room was carpeted with kids. When I asked them what they wanted, they responded, 'Everything!' I prayed for them to know Jesus, to know the fullness of the gifts and the fruit and the power of the Holy Spirit. Because of time and language limitations, I told them I was going to lift up Jesus the crucified One who is the power of God and the wisdom of God. I told them I was going to bless them with 'Three-in-One' oil — Father, Son and Holy Spirit. I told them we would lift up Jesus to allow Him to do whatever needed to be done in each life. I lined them up and began blessing them with oil, saying, 'I lift up Jesus.' One by one they went down under the power. We prayed for five hours, and the power of God moved in a way that would baffle the minds of theologians. It was not a problem for me to believe that God would move like that in Germany. The need was so great. When I see this kind of sovereign move of God, in power that is totally baffling and blowing everyone's minds, I simply say, 'It is God moving.'

"I saw God moving with that same kind of power in churches all over Germany. People in the hundreds and hundreds rested in the Spirit, as God just sovereignly did for them whatever needed to be done. There was no way in my natural mind, even if I knew German, that I could even begin to respond to the needs that were there in those people.

"On another occasion back in the States, a sister came to me for prayer. I didn't have time to pray with her, so I said, 'Honey, I don't have time so I will just pray with you and ask God to rest you in His Spirit. Don't get up until you ask God if you can.' So I prayed and she went under the power. Three hours later she came to tell me what happened. She related that she first said to God, 'I'm hungry.' He said, 'Shhhhh. . . .' Then He began giving her visions, one after another, like a movie. Then she asked me, 'What is deliverance?' (She was ignorant of the renewal.) I responded, 'Why do you ask?' She said, 'Because God said that is what is happening to me. I was being delivered from my fears and my angers and my bitterness and resentment.'

"She was being delivered of those things that controlled her, and that was a real teaching for me. Since then when I pray with people to rest in the Spirit I encourage them to know that it can go far beyond the experience of God's power and presence, warmth and gentleness. It can go beyond the positive experiences into a deliverance from the negatives in people's lives."

"Be at rest once more, O my soul, for the Lord has been good to you" (Psalm 116:7).

"When I was praying with families in a neighborhood group, the adults asked me to pray for all the children to rest in the Spirit. As I prayed for them, I noticed one little nine-year-old girl resting sweetly for a long time. When she got up I said to her, 'Honey, did you see Jesus?' She said, 'Yes.' I said, 'What did He say to you?' She looked at me a bit chagrined and shared, 'Jesus asked me if I would like to stop sucking my thumb.'

"When I heard her say that, it was totally confirmed within me that Jesus knows every hidden compulsion in our lives. He not only knows them, but He wants to set us free from that compulsion. We don't have to tell Him. We don't even have to know it as we are prayed for, but Jesus will bring it to our minds. He will say, 'Would you like to stop sucking your thumb? Would you like to be set free from that sex perversion, or that deep buried anger, or whatever controls you?' Having seen it in that little girl, I have seen it in many people of many different ages. He whom the Son sets free is free indeed. Resting is one of the main ways I have seen people come into freedom from the powers of darkness, especially those controlled by bitterness, anger or depression."[30]

". . . Stand firm and you will see the deliverance the Lord will bring you today . . ." (Exodus 14:13).

AREN'T YOU GLAD WE ASKED? . . .
statistics continued

9. Have you rested in the Spirit when no one prayed on you?

Yes	50%
No	47%
Not answered	3%

(The breakdown reflects a higher percentage of women than men resting when no one prayed on them. The figures show 43% of the men saying "yes" compared with 50% of the women.)

10. Have you rested in the Spirit while alone?

Yes	41%
No	54%
Not answered	5%

11. Are you aware of any major healing while resting in the Spirit?

Yes	54%
No	41%
Not answered	5%

(Figures for male and female are comparable.)

. . . to be continued

Review of Key Points

Father Jack Soulsby

* We need to be open to the gift of resting in the Spirit, and also desire it.

* It is important to integrate theory with personal experience and witness.

Father Robert Voigt

* The Holy Spirit can work well with us when we are relaxed.

* When faith is weak, we need extra gifts, such as resting in the Spirit.

* The increase of faith and love that come with resting can be of great value.

* Resting should only be done in believing groups.

Sister Carmen Parilla

* We need to be open to receive healing, whether we rest or not.

* Most people who go down will be healed in some way because they have released and opened themselves to His healing power.

Father Ralph DiOrio

* When people gather in the presence of the Holy Spirit, God touches them powerfully.

* Dusty, unused faith can be activated in an affirming atmosphere.

* Testimonies of healing help us believe that God is alive.

Father John Kenny

* We must experience resting in the Spirit before we make any personal judgments.

Father Rick Thomas

* The most incorrigible people can be melted by the love of Jesus.

Bishop Donald Montrose

* I don't believe resting in the Spirit is beneficial for large groups.

* In general there seems to be interior healing and greater peace with resting in the Spirit.

* Negative influences can manifest with resting in the Spirit.

Father Tom McCormick

* Jesus often moves in power while people rest in the Spirit.

* We need to be careful of abuses.

* There is a great need for pastoring and teaching in this area.

* We need to focus on the giver of the gift.

Father James McManus

* We shouldn't necessarily equate the physical experience of falling with the action of the Spirit.

* I prefer not to minister in such a way to facilitate the experience.

* I have experienced great peacefulness and prayerfulness while resting in the Spirit.

Sister Francis Clare

* I ask Jesus to rest people in the Spirit when I sense Him wanting to take over.

* Jesus delivers people from negatives in their lives while resting people in the Spirit.

* He wants to set us free from controlling influences.

Prayer

Heavenly Father, I want to yield to You at a deeper level. With Father Jack Soulsby, I want to be open to resting in the Spirit. With Father Robert Voigt, I want to focus on the upbuilding of faith. With Sister Carmen Parilla, I desire to be open to Your healing power. With the people in Father Ralph DiOrio's stories, I want to experience miracles, healings and freedom from hangups. With the inmates in Father Rick Thomas' stories, I want to be moved so deeply that I weep on my knees, and experience change of heart. With Bishop Donald Montrose, I want a balance of openness and appropriate caution. With Father Tom McCormick, I want to focus on the giver of

the gift. With Father James McManus, I want a gift of prayerfulness. And with Sister Francis Clare, I want to be totally open to Your sovereign move in my life. Thank You, Heavenly Father. Thank You, Jesus. Thank You, Holy Spirit. Amen.

"(I pray) that the God of our Lord Jesus Christ, the Glorious Father, may give you the Spirit of wisdom and revelation, so that you may know Him better. I pray also that the eyes of your heart may be enlightened in order that you may know the hope to which He has called you, the riches of His glorious inheritance in the saints, and His incomparably great power for us who believe . . ." (Ephesians 1:17-19).

5

He Leads Me in Paths of Righteousness for His Name's Sake

"O Lord, You have searched me and You know me. You know when I sit and when I rise; You perceive my thoughts from afar. You discern my going out and my lying down; You are familiar with all my ways" (Psalm 139:1-3).

In this section we will share some thoughts about the interplay of psychological dynamics with resting in the Spirit. Health care professionals will respond to some questions from a survey, make a few recommendations and share personal experiences.

"You Discern My Lying Down . . ."
Some Controversial Areas

Some leaders in the renewal have a concern that resting in the Spirit is not activated by the Holy Spirit, but is, rather, a mixture. The author of an article in *New Covenant* comments on this viewpoint:

> ". . . Other people have some reservations about the phenomenon. They see the experience as all too similar to states of hypnosis and auto-suggestion which are not necessarily connected

with the Holy Spirit. They seriously question the scriptural basis of the phenomenon and have grave reservations about the pastoral wisdom of encouraging it."[31]

Cardinal Suenens in *A Controversial Phenomenon, Resting in the Spirit,*[32] concludes that the tendency to fall could relate more to psychological dynamics than the movement of the Holy Spirit, and thus issues a caution.

I tend to believe that most (but not all) resting is an experience of Jesus. Father Richard Bain of San Francisco shares his thoughts in this regard:

> "It may be true that most resting in the Spirit is caused by psychological dynamics. Maybe a lot of people just want to go down. I don't think that is a matter of real concern, though, because when they are down they may become open to being touched by God. The issue in my mind is not so much why they go down, but what happens to them when they are down.
>
> "The Church is not God, the sacraments are not God. The rosary isn't God. But each sets up the dynamics to help us encounter God. I believe resting in the Spirit can also help us encounter God. Everyone I have talked with has found it a very positive experience.
>
> "My first experience of resting, with Father Dennis Kelleher of New York, opened the door to my healing ministry."[33]

There is probably a mixture of psychological and spiritual dynamics in resting in the Spirit, because of the interconnectedness of body, mind and spirit. Father George Maloney in an article, "How to Understand and Evaluate the Charismatics' Latest Experience: 'Slaying in the

Spirit,' " states: "The phenomenon of slaying in the Spirit is not to be judged on an either/or basis: whether it is 'natural' or 'supernatural,' induced by man's psychic nature alone, or completely a demonstration of the Holy Spirit's power among men. . . ."[34]

Another common area of controversy is concerned with "spontaneous" resting versus "induced, cooperative or ministered resting." Spontaneous resting is not generally criticized. The area of conflict deals with what is acceptable in terms of encouraging people to open up to the resting experience, with "induced, cooperative or ministered resting." The conflict emerges when psychological dynamics are involved in the resting process.

I believe helping people move into a position of yielding to God is a positive, constructive act. One might ask the question, "Towards what are they yielding their heart? What is their intent?" Peter made the move in the natural to walk on the water (Matthew 14:29), and then the Lord took over. The Lord says, *"Come, all you who are thirsty . . ."* (Isaiah 55:1). He says, *"Come . . . and I will give you rest . . ."* (Matthew 11:28). That initial coming is a natural act in response to His call. He is always calling us to yield, and then as we do, He moves us into the spiritual realm. In the gift of tongues, we open our physical mouths and He gives the spiritual utterance. He tells us to stir up the gifts. That is a natural act in the initial stage. We make an internal choice to shift from functioning in the natural realm to functioning in the spiritual realm. As we decide to yield, in trust, we are saying, "Take me, Lord, into Your House." He honors our choice.

Over the years I have been comfortable with praying over people and encouraging them to be open and yielded to the Holy Spirit. There are some thoughts along this line that may prove helpful:

1. Many Catholics are afraid of external religious experience, immediately placing it in the category of "emotionalism." Some observers have said that we need emotions in our faith to give balance to the intellectual dimension. St. Augustine says: "faith seeking understanding." We need to open our hearts to the Lord's love and power.

2. Most people are unable to fall on their backs unprotected, naturally speaking. When people have questioned resting, I have asked them to fall backwards unprotected, and none of them have been able to do so. Under the power of the Holy Spirit, people do that which is ordinarily impossible.

3. Many who fall under the power of the Spirit are educated, professional people whose last desire is to be on the ground. Even very prim and proper people seem to lose that concern as they rest in the Spirit.

4. Seek the community discernment process. We are told in 1 John 4:1 to *"test the spirits."* The community, the prayer ministers and the ones receiving prayer usually have a pretty good sense of the presence or absence of the Lord during prayer ministry. Most often the community will sense the presence of the Holy Spirit during the resting process.

5. Many priests in full-time healing ministries are in agreement about the good fruit that comes with resting in the Spirit. The bishops who have attended these services, and sometimes rested themselves, give added support to this aspect of the healing ministry.

6. Our God is a God of surprises. We need to be

open to the ways in which the Spirit may be leading the Body. When the dark gets darker, the light gets lighter. With all of the evil on the rise in our day, we need to become even more yielded to the leading of the Lord. He tells us, *". . . let your light shine before men, that they may see your good deeds and praise your Father in heaven"* (Matthew 5:16).

7. We should presume on the basic honesty and integrity of people, until proven otherwise. Some would say that not everyone who falls is resting in the Spirit. That is probably true, but I would presume that the vast majority of them are under the power of the Spirit. For this reason, I am comfortable with using that terminology.

8. Most phenomena are subject to use and abuse. I have known people who have fasted too much and hurt their health. Occasionally one finds parents who go to daily Mass to the neglect of their family. However, we focus on the use rather than the abuse.

9. Good order and decency should always be preserved. I think that pastorally we should check and stop any abuse, such as letting oneself rest in the Spirit while receiving Holy Communion, or in the middle of a Sunday Mass, or in a public place. Manifestly, these are abuses and should be pastorally corrected.

"Hypnosis, Hysteria and Resting Therapy . . ."
MD's and Psychologists Respond to Survey

In the survey (see Appendix) 10 psychologists and 12 medical doctors who have personally rested in the Spirit shared their views. When asked whether they viewed resting in the Spirit as mass hysteria or hypnosis, they responded as follows:

Seven of the ten psychologists responded that in their opinion, resting in the Spirit was neither hypnosis nor mass hysteria. Some of the qualifications on that answer included:

* "Partly a trance-like state."
* "More mass hysteria than hypnosis. As more go down the tendency to rest increases."
* "My own experience underscores my belief in its validity."
* "I'm very resistant to hypnosis and have no hysterical symptoms in my psychological history."

Two of the psychologists did not respond to the specific question about mass hysteria or hypnosis, but said the following in the "comments" section:

* "A hypnotic component with or without hysteria."
* "Brainwave could be close to that of hypnosis."

Eight of the twelve medical doctors specifically commented that it was neither mass hysteria nor hypnosis. Two qualified their answers as follows:

* "More the power of expectation and suggestion than a true work of the Spirit."
* "True resting in the Spirit is not hypnosis or mass hysteria, but there are times when it seems 'in' to rest, and that is a problem."

Two physicians did not specifically answer the question, but made the following comments:

* "It could be both hypnosis and mass hysteria."
* "It can be hypnosis and mass hysteria and is, on many occasions."

I asked the psychologists if they would recommend resting in the Spirit as therapeutic. Eight of the ten psychologists said "yes," with the following reasons given:

* "In a general sense, every touch of the Spirit has healing in its rays. The disposition of the person is often a key, I believe. When the person is surrendered, receptive and not controlling the outcome, I think it is therapeutic. Otherwise, I doubt its validity. The real thing is by nature therapeutic."

* "Well, I experienced a powerful healing."

* "The freedom from defenses and anxieties can allow the Lord to move in a relatively unhindered manner."

* "Because it brings peace. However, proper education of the non-initiated patient is quite necessary."

* "The Lord takes over the process and more is accomplished than would happen with plain therapy."

One psychologist was uncertain about recommending resting in the Spirit as therapeutic because he felt it was "essentially unpredictable; that it may or may not produce healing."

One psychologist would not recommend resting as therapeutic because, "It is too soon to say how therapeutic it is. It feels so good, so people want to repeat it, but I'm not so sure it is therapeutic."

Six of the twelve medical doctors recommended resting in the Spirit as therapeutic for the following reasons:

* "Precisely because I believe with all my heart that the Lord touches us deeply when we surrender deeply."

* "One sees things in proper perspective."

* "This is a healing process. It should be for that purpose."
* "Minimally, it is very relaxing, soothing and uplifting."
* "It is healing prayer."
* "Because a controlling attitude is a hindrance to spiritual growth."

Four of the medical doctors were "uncertain" about recommending resting. One added a comment that, "It is not something to seek, but to leave to God."

One physician stated that he would "neither recommend for or against resting in the Spirit."

". . . the Lord blesses His people with peace" (Psalm 29:11).

"Consider This . . ." Additional Reflections From Psychologists and Medical Doctors

* "There is a long history to this phenomenon."
* "It is one of God's many means of ministering to us."
* "It is merely an outward sign of releasing your body to the Lord, as you release your inner self to Him."
* "It is nothing to be afraid of. There is no need to fear yielding to the Holy Spirit."
* "Receive it as a gift of God; a ministry of God. It is not a gift from a person."
* "There are psychological aspects, and human energies can play a part in the experience."
* "It can't be taught through action or effort."
* "Be open, but do not strive for it."
* "You don't have to do or expect anything."

* "It is the power of the Holy Spirit, not of man, at work. It is God's power, and God's work. Therefore, relax and let Him work."
* "It is an invitation to surrender totally to God."
* "Give up conscious control while resting, in order to let the Lord lead."
* "Let it flow from God."
* "Keep your focus on Jesus."
* "There are many experiences of resting with both specific and general results."
* "The level of healing at these moments ordinarily is a very deep, foundational level."
* "Even if there are no signs, God is present."
* "It promotes freedom to be yourself."
* "It heals."
* "Not everyone is free enough to receive it — through no fault of their own."
* "It is not necessary to rest in the Spirit to be touched by the Spirit."

Testimonies

"I've Been Hypnotized Many Times . . ."
A Florida Psychiatrist Compares Notes

"Being a psychiatrist, I deal with psychological phenomena such as collective hysteria. I have also been hypnotized several times for different reasons. I went to Father DeGrandis' services because my daughter prompted me, knowing I was not doing well. I was depressed and not happy with my life at all, and she thought that going to a charismatic group would help me not to feel so lonely.

"How can I differentiate the resting experience from

93

mass hysteria? I can begin to tell from the talk and behavior of the people. This was a totally different experience. There were 200-300 people at this service. We were lined up to be anointed, and since the place was so big I had no idea of what was happening at the wall on the other side. Because my eyes were closed I had no idea of when Father DeGrandis was going to be near me. I kept singing religious songs very softly until I felt something pushing me backwards. I simply let myself go. I knew I was lying on the floor, but I felt like I was floating on the air. I felt a great sense of relief, and peace. At some point I felt waves of heat moving from my feet to my head. At no moment did I feel any contact with Father DeGrandis, and at no time did I feel his physical presence near me. I got up when I wanted to get up, and was very surprised at feeling so peaceful.

"The difference between this experience and being hypnotized is that on the many occasions that I was hypnotized I was always in contact with the person who hypnotized me. I was always following certain commands and was told what to do when I woke up.

"Resting in the Spirit was a beautiful experience that I like to share with other people."

"Marinated and Ready . . ." A Wisconsin MD Shares

"When I first heard about resting in the Spirit I thought it was silly, dramatic and put-on. Then I was just embarrassed and nervous. I doubted that it would happen to me. When it did happen, I 'floated' down and laid in a peaceful, blissful and freeing atmosphere of light.

"On the short term, I feel that resting in the Spirit is a rapid way to be freed of burdens and anxieties. It sort of marinates me and readies me for what the Lord wants to do.

"On the long term, I see a great deal of inner healing. Each time I was brought closer to the Father through Jesus. In my mind's eye, while I was down I saw Jesus take me as a little boy, then adolescent, then young adult, to the present time, and bring me before the Father. He held me on His lap each time. This has provided much self-worth, self-acceptance and affirmation."

"Overwhelming Love . . ."
Letter From a Louisiana Doctor

"Dear Father DeGrandis:

"May I share with you an experience of God's overwhelming love? After your forgiveness prayer at the weekend retreat I prayed earnestly for my deceased father, who had been an alcoholic. For many years I had avoided looking like or being like Daddy. I was ashamed of him. As I stood in the communion line at Mass on the retreat, I felt myself looking like Daddy. Far from wanting to change this, I felt very comfortable. Somehow for the first time I understood him and his goodness. I was proud to be like him.

"When I was standing in the circle waiting for the anointing, I thought about the six weeks we were committing ourselves to pray the forgiveness prayer, and wondered if I should ask the Lord for some suffering to offer up for Daddy while I said the prayer. At that instant an inner voice said, 'This will not be necessary, Joe, I have suffered it already.' Then you anointed me and I rested in the Spirit. I could not stop crying as I encountered once again, the Lord's overwhelming love."

"God, I Feel Dumb Lying Here — I'm a Doctor . . ."
Testimony of a Holy Spirit Overhaul

Sister Francis Clare shares the following story:
"I remember praying with a group once that included a doctor. The doctor came up afterwards to testify about what happened. He said he thought he'd never go down under the power, so he felt very secure in coming up for prayer. The next thing he knew, he was on the floor. He testified, 'The first thing I did was ask God if I could get up. God said, "No." A little time went by, and I said, "God, can I get up now?" God still said, "No." The third time around I said, "God, I feel dumb lying here, I'm a doctor." God replied, "Feel dumb." ' When he finally let go and said, 'Okay, God, do what You have to do,' then God's power began to work on him. He shared, 'I got a complete overhaul.' And when you are a doctor, you know when you are being overhauled!"

"Once when a priest was praying for me he started to go down. It took all of my strength to keep him in the vertical position!" (medical doctor).

AREN'T YOU GLAD WE ASKED? . . .
  statistics continued

12. Do you feel that resting in the Spirit has been
    a gift from the Lord for you?
        Yes   94%
        No   2%
        Not answered   4%

    (The figure for male and female are nearly
    identical.)

13. Has it helped your prayer life, as far as you
    know?
        Yes   82%
        No   13%
        Not answered   5%

14. Has it helped you experience the presence of
    the Lord in your daily life?
        Yes   86%
        No   5%
        Not answered   9%

(Male and female figures are comparable.)

                                . . . to be continued

Review of Key Points

* There are two schools of thought about the cause
  and value of resting in the Spirit.

* One view holds that it is a gift of God for healing
  and empowerment.

* Another view cautions that resting could have psychological or even demonic origins or aspects.

* There is likely a mixture of psychological and spiritual dynamics in the experience of resting in the Spirit.

* The Lord can touch us as deeply as we yield to Him.

* Emotional eruptions can occur as we are set free from deep wounds and evil spirits possibly brought in by those wounds.

* When a person is surrendered, receptive and not controlling the outcome, resting in the Spirit can be therapeutic.

* Resting can free a person from defenses.

* The Lord can touch us deeply when we surrender deeply.

* A controlling attitude in a person can be a hindrance to spiritual growth.

* When we rest and allow the Lord to take over the healing process, more may be accomplished than in plain therapy.

Prayer

Heavenly Father, please reveal any hidden motivations and psychic influence in my experience of resting in the Spirit. With the Florida psychiatrist, the Wisconsin doctor and the Louisiana MD, I want to deeply encounter You. With them, I want to be lifted beyond the confines of any depression, childhood wounds and poor self-image to receive

a "Holy Spirit overhaul."

Heavenly Father, make me into a pure and powerful instrument of releasing this gift in others. Let those for whom I pray come into a life-changing experience of Your love. Thank You, Heavenly Father. Thank You, Lord Jesus. Thank You, Holy Spirit. Amen.

"The Lord will fulfill His purpose for me . . ." (Psalm 138:8).

6

I Will Fear No Evil, for You Are With Me

"As the mountains surround Jerusalem, so the Lord surrounds His people, both now and evermore" (Psalm 125:2).

Not everyone is free enough internally to yield to the experience of resting in the Spirit. Francis MacNutt reflects on this lack of freedom:

"There are certain types of people who seem to block this experience — notably those who lead lives where they have overcontrolled their emotions. Some people are really afraid to let go. It isn't so much of a spiritual problem as an emotional one; they are afraid of anything they can't control through their reason . . . some people have lost their ability to respond to life with spontaneity."[35]

Often, intellectual people will have a harder time resting in the Spirit, although this was not the case with my former seminary Scripture teacher. He is a man who holds a licentiate in sacred scripture from the Jerusalem Biblical Institute, and a Ph.D. in psychology. The first time he was prayed over, he instantly fell under the power of the Spirit, with great openness. He is very learned, and yet has a great openness. This is unusual.

Generally, I think the type of people who rest more

readily are those who are free, open, daring and yielding. Usually they are people with a measure of simplicity. The more intellectual, reserved, conservative types tend to experience more resistance to resting in the Spirit. It seems, then, that there is a need for psychological openness as well as spiritual openness.

In this section we will examine and pray about some of the ways that people are blocked from resting in the Spirit. A number of pastoral concerns will be revealed and some suggestions will be given to help individuals before, during and after the experience.

Dorothea's List of Psychological Barriers to Resting in the Spirit

In her inner healing ministry my sister, Dorothea De-Grandis Sudol, has come to recognize a number of blockages that can interfere with resting in the Spirit. They include:
* Skeptical attitude
* Intellectual approach to religion
* Fear of the unknown
* Fear of falling
* Fear of fainting
* Fear of loss of control
* Lack of desire
* Fear of closeness to God
* Fear of yielding
* Physical impairment (i.e., epileptic seizure, need for a cane, etc.)
* Fearful association with being on back (sickness, surgery, rape)
* Serious emotional trauma connected with death of others

* Lack of trust in God
* Lack of trust in people
* Embarrassed by size of body
* Pregnancy (fear of hurting unborn child)
* Feeling of unworthiness
* Fear of mystical experience[36]

Prayer to Remove Barriers:

Heavenly Father, please release me from all barriers to resting in the Spirit. Dissolve any roots of skepticism, cynicism, or intellectual resistance. Send Your love into the roots of every fear, embarrassment and insecurity. Touch any lack of trust. Help me to draw close and open my heart to You. In Jesus' name. Amen.

". . . where the Spirit of the Lord is, there is freedom" (2 Corinthians 3:17).

Inviting the Lord deeply into the root of the problem area, and (through forgiveness) releasing Him to work on our behalf, can bring freedom. Everything He touches, He redeems.

Summary of a Few Pastoral Concerns

One eminent person has said of resting in the Spirit, that there are no theological problems, but there are many pastoral problems. I tend to agree with that statement. A few of the basic areas include:

WHERE TO USE IT: I think we need to be careful where we allow resting in the Spirit to occur. I would not use it at a parish mission, for example, or at any non-charismatic church services. Ideally it should be used primarily in private and counseling situations. It could also be used at charismatic healing services.

NEED FOR TEACHING: This is extremely important. When I am getting ready to anoint and pray, I always announce that some individuals may go down on the floor. The people need to be told that this is an ordinary experience and they don't need to call an ambulance or send a doctor. Some people have prayed over large groups of people without even mentioning what could happen. People would fall under the power of the Spirit, observers would be shocked and dismayed and leave the gathering. In our society when we see people fall down we think they are in distress or having a heart attack. We need to forewarn people about what can happen, and give them a sense of what to expect, both externally and internally, just as a doctor or a dentist generally forewarns a patient about an upcoming procedure.

Sometimes we need to help people make room in their minds for resting in the Spirit to occur. This allows them to do what they are already prompted to do by the Holy Spirit.

Some people who don't rest in the Spirit will feel left out or feel that God doesn't love them. They need to be reassured of God's love. They also may need more teaching and prayer to help them become more psychologically open to the experience. Reassure people that the absence of resting in the Spirit doesn't mean they aren't close to God. Equally we must say that resting is not a sign of holiness. While Mother Teresa of Calcutta has probably never rested in the Spirit, I know some definite scoundrels who have rested.

RESTING CAN BE CONTROLLED: The act of falling is generally under the control of the person who is resting. If you are holding charismatic services at a facility that does not readily lend itself to resting in the Spirit, or in an inappropriate situation, tell the participants to close off their spirits to the experience, and ask them not to rest. You will find in most cases if they will do that, there will be no resting. I asked about 700 people in a small church in Brisbane, Australia, to refrain from resting by closing their spirits to the experience because the circumstances were inappropriate. They did, successfully.

NEGATIVE EXPERIENCES: From my experience I would say that negative activity while resting is infrequent. Individuals who worry about negative activity happening usually have inadequate experience with or understanding about the negative forces from which individuals are being set free. Sometimes in these cases, painful memories or evil spirits are being replaced by the presence of Jesus, and what may appear negative is actually a positive thing. Often the evil spirits are brought in by, or tied into, deep emotional wounds, so there can be a strong release of emotions during the healing process. Francis MacNutt says: ". . . anything which is not simple and peaceful is not the direct action of the Spirit, but is the reaction of wounded human nature or the forces of evil."[37]

When an individual who is resting seems to be stirred up or agitated in some way, a mature, trained counselor (with some knowledge of spiritual warfare and inner healing prayer) should be dispatched to minister to the person.

SPACE CONSIDERATIONS: In a group there should be ample space provided for people to rest on the floor.

USHERS: Make sure there are good, trained ushers to keep everything in good order, with a quiet and reverent atmosphere.

CATCHERS: There should be trained catchers to stand behind the individuals being prayed over to carefully ease them to the floor. If they do rest, always be sure there is a catcher before you start to pray over a particular person. They should also be watchful to help people get up when they are ready.

MUSIC: I believe in the value of having a good music ministry playing charismatic songs during the time people are resting in the Spirit. This helps folks focus on Jesus in deep praise, which in turn opens them to deeper surrender.

TESTIMONY AFTER THE EXPERIENCE: After resting in the Spirit it would be good to have testimonies from the people about what they have experienced, so that what is taught can be seen and validated in the experience of the people. There are three questions that might help in individual assessment:

1. Was it valuable?
2. Did it meet a need?
3. Has a deeper experience of God occurred?

Only the person who has experienced it can truly say if this has happened. You will be amazed at the depth of the experience in many people. In my mind, the depth of satisfaction accompanying the experience is an indication of its authenticity. This needs to be shared.

INFORMATIONAL MATERIALS: There should be hand-out sheets of local resources, including lists of local prayer groups and suggested reading materials for growth.

FOLLOW UP: I believe there should be mature, trained people to do follow up. People with negative experiences, especially, should have on-going prayer counseling. Getting deep areas stirred up, with no follow-up, is a matter of genuine pastoral concern. Generally, I will only conduct services where there is a prayer group to follow up and put people in a loving community that can continue the healing process.

HANDLING ABUSE: All of us are aware that there

can be use and abuse of anything. All gifts can be abused, which is why they need the guidance and discernment of teachers and pastors. Resting in the Spirit can be used for good and it can be abused. For example, one person going to three different people to be prayed over can be an abuse. Focusing on the minister of the gift instead of Jesus can be an abuse. Excessive attachment to the external experience rather than the internal experience can be an abuse. (It indicates a lack of understanding of the central core of the experience, and is thus a signal of the need for teaching.) Prayer ministers who are on an ego trip about being able to rest people in the Spirit can abuse the gift. I think it is the concern of those in the teaching ministry to set up guidelines and to counsel, so that abuses can be corrected.

"Before, During and After . . ."
Preparing to Enter His Rest

As I mention in *The Healing Ministry,* I would:

". . . suggest to some who perhaps have never rested in the Spirit and want to grow in the love of the Lord, that you might ask the Lord to let them rest in the Spirit. People say, 'I want it,' but if they desire it only with their minds and not their hearts, they ordinarily will not receive. If you open yourself, then the door to your heart opens from the inside. Tell the Lord, 'I want to receive everything you've got for me, Lord. I want to receive everything which will make me a better person, one who loves You more, serves You more and other people more.' "[38]

Sister Francis Clare makes the following recommendations:

BEFORE THE EXPERIENCE: "Do not make anything happen and do not prevent His power from coming upon you by being frightened about where you will fall and how you will look and what people will think about you. Release yourself from any of these fears. Relax in His love and gently praise Him for loving you. Release yourself from all guilt feelings about not being worthy. This is not an experience for the worthy; it is for those who need release, inner healing and infilling."

DURING THE EXPERIENCE: "Relax in His love. Surrender to His love. Believe in deep faith that something is happening in you even though you do not feel it emotionally. Stay in the position of relaxation as long as you feel you should."

AFTER THE EXPERIENCE: "When returning to the normal level of mind-consciousness, silence inside of you any thoughts of self-condemnation, self-analysis, what people will think, disappointments that you didn't feel anything. Remaining in the resting experience for five minutes or five hours is not a sign of greater sinfulness or greater holiness. Words of love and worship to the Father, to the Son and to the Holy Spirit from your sincere heart keep the healing flowing in the heart continuously. Be open to living in God's will every day. This experience of resting in the Spirit is only a beginning. The Lord will continue His work throughout the hours to come in the remaining week, month and maybe even years. That He would want to love us and let His Precious Blood cleanse us in this way is indeed a great joy.

"Jesus is the Healer and His Holy Spirit ef-

fects the healing because the Father wants it at this
moment in your life.''

Testimonies

"It Struck Me as Too Simple . . ."
Sister Monica's Forgiveness Story

"In 1979, shortly after I joined a monastery, I had
adjustment problems based on an unhealed relationship
with my mother. She was mentally ill, but I and the rest
of my family didn't yet realize that fact.

"My spiritual director sent me to see a priest in the
healing ministry, Father Joe Otte. The instant I saw him,
I trusted him totally. He led me in a simple dialogue of
forgiveness with my mother (which struck me as too simple to affect such a deep problem). Then he stood up to
pray over me. He did not touch me, and I had never heard
of 'resting in the Spirit.' I soon found I had no strength
to stand, and was flat on the floor. As I lay there he began
to speak, but his voice sounded miles away. He told me
to go through the forgiveness dialogue with everyone I
had trouble with, and not to get up until I sensed the process was complete. I felt an enormous sense of well being
and peace, and after about 45 minutes felt ready to get up.

"Shortly after that experience I received news that my
mother had to be institutionalized as psychotic, and I flew
to Michigan to help her with the transition. She immediately began lashing out at me in old destructive patterns
that had angered me so much in the past, but this time
I was completely free of anger. All of my childhood love
for her returned, and her love for me then began to be
released also. A 27-year-old wound was healed, and remained healed until the day she died.

"My mother had been deeply involved in the occult world, and the occult had also played a part in my life before my conversion. If I had heard of resting in the Spirit or seen it happen to someone else, I might have believed it was occult, and would have warned people against it. The quality of Christian life that Father Otte displayed and the fruits of that experience have, together, convinced me that it is a genuine gift of the Holy Spirit, and not an activity of occult spirits. It is the Holy Spirit that brought freedom and love back into my relationship with my mother, and He did it through 'resting in the Spirit.' "

"Be at rest once more, O my soul, for the Lord has been good to you" (Psalm 116:7).

"I Even Tried Pizza . . ." A Canadian Report

"Dear Father DeGrandis:

"A few years ago if I just heard about healing services I would run away. Then gradually as I came to know the Lord and with the help of people around me, my attitude changed. Over the last two years I have been anointed many times and never experienced being 'slain' or 'resting' in the Spirit. I always wanted to, but inwardly was fearful and I held back from being completely open to God's healing.

"At your healing service at church, when you felt the presence of healing in certain people, I was wishing for healing of my stomach and chest problems that had been with me for a few months. I was taking medication but nothing helped. I had prayed, but felt no answer. That night I felt nothing at all when you had words of knowledge about the Lord healing people.

"Then, before the anointing, when you explained how

to be open to the power of the Holy Spirit,* I decided to try it. I sang loudly and I raised my hands. Even though I didn't trust enough to close my eyes, I knew that the Holy Spirit was moving powerfully. It happened so fast. I felt the warm sensation on my forehead as you anointed me. Everything became very peaceful. I don't know how to explain the rest, but it was beautiful.

"I went home that night wondering if I could play 'hooky' from work the next day, so I could go to your workshop. I just craved for more. I sang all night in my heart, and even into the next day.

"That night I was healed of my stomach and chest problems. Thursday and Friday passed. Saturday came and my appetite came back. I even tried pizza to test this whole thing out. To date I still don't have the pain. It's great not only to receive physical healing, but also to know God loves me. Now I can allow God to lead me to be more loving and forgiving of others."

"May the peoples praise You, O God; may all the peoples praise You" (Psalm 67:3).

"The Gentle Call of Jesus . . ." Tom's Testimony

"For ten years I was involved with selling and using drugs, primarily marijuana and cocaine. I was an addict, and all I wanted was to get stoned. I was raised as a Christian, but all those values were stripped away during this terrifying time. I had no control over my life. I was frightened, helpless and unable to break away. One night after

*You might want to refer back to the statistics on healing on page 55. Also, on page 19, note that 62% of the people who had rested had received an explanation. It would be interesting in a future study to see if there is a relationship between receiving an explanation and healings received.

a party, I became desperate. I crawled to a crucifix above my bed and asked God to please help me.

"A week later I went to my parish church and visited the Holy Eucharist. I begged for God's help. As the days rolled by I felt the gentle call of Jesus to go to confession. When I did go, I was so ashamed of my drug problem that I didn't tell the priest. While I was sitting at the tabernacle after confession I decided to go back and confess my drug involvements and addiction. The priest was so pleased with my return. As he raised his hand to bless me, a strange, joyful numbness came over my body, from my head to my feet. I came to understand later that I was resting in the Spirit while sitting in the chair. My legs were like rubber as I made my way to the car after confession.

"I was overwhelmed by the physical experience of God's love. I was certain that He was pleased with me, and that He loved me very much. This direct, personal knowledge of His love gave me the strength I needed to recover from the addiction, and helped me let go of seeking unhealthy experiences.

"Through resting in the Spirit the Lord revealed a new life to me. I am now a prayer group leader with a heart for loving and serving God's people."

"I will give them a heart to know me . . ." (Jeremiah 24:7).

AREN'T YOU GLAD WE ASKED? . . .
statistics concluded

15. Do you think it is appropriate for a Catholic to rest in the Spirit in charismatic services or prayer groups?

Yes	91%
No	2%
Not answered	7%

16. Would you encourage others to have this experience?

Yes	90%
No	2%
Not answered	8%

(The figures indicate a higher number of men than women willing to encourage others to rest in the Spirit, with 96% of the men saying "yes" compared with 88% of the women saying "yes.")

17. Would you like to see it an ordinary part of Catholic life?

Yes	87%
No	3%
Not answered	10%

(On this question also, the men's "yes" response is higher at 94% compared with 85% of the women.)

(end of survey)

"Lord . . . You made us for Yourself, and our hearts are restless until they rest in You" (Confessions of St. Augustine).

Review of Key Points

* Some people have lost the ability to respond to life with spontaneity.

* God wants to set us free from those things that block our ability to freely yield to Him.

* For those who have deep, painful areas stirred up during resting, it is important to have responsible follow-up.

* We need the guidance and discernment of pastors and teachers to resolve areas of abuse.

Prayer

Heavenly Father, please renew in me the ability to respond to life with freedom and spontaneity. With Sister Monica, I may need new freedom and love in family relationships. With the Canadian I may need a deeper knowledge of Your healing love. With Tom, I continue to need the strength that comes from a deep knowledge of Your love.

Heavenly Father, as a leader I need to grow in pastoral wisdom. Freedom and safe guidelines are both necessary in the experience of resting in the Spirit. Thank You for maturing me in these areas. In Jesus' name. Amen.

". . . I have come that they may have life, and have it to the full" (John 10:10).

7

He Anoints My Head With Oil; My Cup Overflows

"May the God of hope fill you with all joy and peace as you trust in Him, so that you may overflow with hope by the power of the Holy Spirit" (Romans 15:13).

A 27-year-old woman came up to me after a service one time and said of her resting experience: "Father, that was the best experience of my life." I countered, "You mean the best religious experience." She responded, "No, I mean the best experience!"

God is love, and He longs to have us experience that love. As I travel and minister around the country and in other countries, I see Christians united in their longing for a deep experience of Jesus. It is one thing to hear about His love. It is another thing to tangibly experience it. It is one thing to hear that God heals. It is another thing to feel His direct, holy medicine on your own physical body.

Resting in the Spirit seems to be a tremendous aid to the healing ministry. Francis MacNutt says, "I have seen every kind of healing take place while people were resting in the Spirit."[39] I have to agree with him. It seems to be God's modern-day vehicle for moving us into a position to be healed.

This final section will include a few more stories and a brief review of some of the fruit of resting in the Spirit.

Testimonies

"Stay Away From Me, I Haven't Rested . . ."
A California Story

"I had a sudden, overwhelming physical attraction to a man who was traveling with our group to a conference. The desire was mutual, and complicated by the fact that I was married. On the return trip when I was sitting alone in the back of the airplane, a person from the group began giving a powerful prophecy. As I listened, the Spirit of God moved in a mighty way over the whole group, and I rested in the Spirit. As I rested, all sexual desire and frustration instantly disappeared. I rejoiced in sharing this freedom with the man in question. He backed off, however, and responded, 'Stay away from me! I haven't rested!' "

"I Felt Like a Walnut, Opened Up . . ." Luci's Story

"I remember in particular one time I was deeply touched by the Lord while resting in the Spirit. I was the music ministry leader at Father DeGrandis' all day workshop. Throughout the day I felt unrest and an inner, broken feeling that I could not identify. As Father DeGrandis began anointing people at the end of the day, I could not bear it any longer. I knew I must be anointed. As I rested in the Spirit following his anointing, some of my past life came before me. The little child — my little child of the past — was before me, broken and crying

115

within. After resting I asked for prayer. As I rested a second time I felt like a walnut opened to its two halves — the little child and the adult me. I was for the first time in my life in touch with the little child within me who had suffered from sexual abuse. For the first time I could call it by name. From that day on I have pursued inner healing. I have lost sixty pounds and have begun to feel good about myself. I now work with a team in an inner healing ministry.''

"The Back of Jimmy's Shirt . . ." Linda's Story

"There has been a pattern of traumatic events all throughout my life — horror stories that have left deep, bold imprints on my mind. I seemed to be a magnet for these experiences.

"After the death of my step-son I was baptized in the Holy Spirit, and encountered the Healer of Memories. Much of the healing I have subsequently received has occurred while I rested in the Spirit. One powerful experience comes to mind, concerning my father.

"When I was eight years old my father's leg was crushed in a logging accident on his redwood lumber mill in the California coastal mountain range. An employee and long-time friend, Jimmy, carried him from the scene of the accident to a vehicle to take him down the mountain to the hospital in Monterey. The visible record of that event was a perfectly formed image of my father's hand, in blood, soaked into the back of Jimmy's cotton shirt. I saw the imprint on his shirt when I returned from the little country school that afternoon. Over the next 35 years, the image of my father's bloody handprint would occasionally reappear in my mind, along with the emotional content of the experience.

"As I rested in the Spirit in a healing service, some 35 years after the experience, I again saw the back of Jimmy's shirt. But this time it was different. Jesus appeared in the vision. He walked over and placed His own nail scarred and bloody hand on the back of Jimmy's shirt, exactly over the imprint of my father's hand. Moments later He lifted His hand, and Dad's bloody imprint was gone.

"As I lay there resting in the Spirit I was aware that all of the pain in that memory was also gone. In its place was a deep, peaceful awareness that the Lord had sovereignly walked back through the years and into the trauma, placing His own imprint on the back of Jimmy's shirt."

"You will surely forget your trouble, recalling it only as waters gone by" (Job 11:16).

"He Carried Mom in His Arms . . ."
Muriel From Massachusetts Remembers

"I attended a healing service with Father DeGrandis shortly after returning from a three-week vacation in Hawaii. While I was away, my mom went to the National Institute of Health in Maryland. She had a severe heart condition and the Institute was her only hope. I went to the service that night with mom on my heart.

"At the end of the service I was working with Jessie at the book table, when I got a sudden urge to go up for the anointing. As I was anointed I felt myself falling back into the arms of a catcher. A tremendous peace came over me as he gently let me down to the floor. I also had the sense of a brilliant light, something like a spotlight, shining on my face. I could even feel the warmth from the light. It could be compared with the heat from the sun,

117

when sunbathing. Suddenly in my mind I saw Jesus in a white robe with a brown cord around His waist. He entered a hospital room. As He approached the bed I saw that the patient on the bed was my mom. At first I thought He was going to heal her of her heart condition, but then I saw Him take her into His arms and carry her out of the room. The bed and the room were left empty, and I felt a coldness come over me. I began to cry. When I returned to the book table, Jessie asked me what was wrong. I shared with her the vision, and told her I felt the Lord was calling mom home. I knew the Lord was allowing me to prepare myself for what was to come. The next day mother went to the Lord."

Reflections on the Fruit of Resting in the Spirit

In 1909 German pastors met in Berlin and sent out a declaration concerning the pentecostal movement. Among other things, they said that the fundamental feature and constraining power in the movement was "the love for Jesus and the desire that He in all respects may fulfill His purpose in and through us."[40]

Today, in the Catholic Charismatic Renewal, I would say the same thing. Our style may be a little different, but the Spirit of Jesus is the same. He is calling each of us, in all of His churches, to a deeper surrender. As we "fall to the earth and die" (John 12:24), we will produce much fruit.

Let's remind ourselves of some of the fruit of resting in the Spirit in just a few of the stories:

* Billy was released of fear (page 18).
* Vince stopped drinking, smoking and living a worldly life and came back to the Catholic Church (page 51).

* The worldwide ministry of Charles and Frances began on the floor (page 34).
* When Irene was touched by His goodness, it changed her life (page 52).
* A retired journeyman machinist was brought closer to the Lord (page 46).
* A school administrator moved into a new level of understanding of spiritual things (page 47).
* A farm laborer found peace with God (page 47).
* A teacher received a teachable spirit (page 49).
* A homemaker was healed in relation to her earthly and heavenly Fathers (page 49).
* A librarian was healed of four dislocated discs (page 50).
* A boy with bone cancer was healed (page 63).
* A nun was healed of unbelief (page 63).
* Jailed delinquents were filled with peace and hope (page 66).
* A Florida psychiatrist found something better than hypnotism (page 93).
* A doctor received a complete overhaul (page 96).

Conclusion

We have arrived at the end of our study, but I see it as just a beginning. As George Washington Carver didn't begin to know all about the peanut, we haven't begun to understand all there is to know about resting in the Spirit. We have separated a lot of the ingredients, and investigated various applications, yet the question we might ask of God, "Why did You make resting in the Spirit?" is still too big for us. It is time, perhaps, to go out, experience it, and find some more effects for ourselves. *"Taste and see that the Lord is good!"* (Psalm 34:8).

119

Prayer

Heavenly Father, we come back into Your little "workshop" and ask again for Your Spirit of Truth. The truth will set us free. Lord, please come upon us with a mighty anointing of Your Spirit. Touch us with Your deep peace, the peace that the world cannot give. Fill us with Your healing love. Send us forth in Your holy power, to open the eyes of the blind and set the captives free. Thank You, Heavenly Father. Thank You, Lord Jesus. Thank You, Holy Spirit. Amen.

"Surely goodness and love will follow me all the days of my life, and I will dwell in the house of the Lord forever" (Psalm 23:6).

Appendix

Survey of Workshop Participants

Two hundred individuals were surveyed at workshops across the country. There were 148 women and 52 men.

When asked how many times they had previously rested, they responded as follows. (These are NOT percentages.)

less than 3 times — 10
3-20 times — 135
21-50 times — 17
51-100 times — 7
over 100 times — 20
no answer — 11

When they were asked how many years they have been in the renewal, they responded as follows:

less than 3 years — 11
3-7 years — 73
7-10 years — 42
over 10 years — 50
no answer — 24

The following questions were asked:
1. Was there an explanation of resting in the Spirit prior to the experience?
2. Were you encouraged to rest in the Spirit?
3. Were you frightened when you rested in the Spirit the first time?
4. Were you surprised at your first experience?
5. Are you aware of any healing when you rested the first time?
6. Are you aware of any healing when you rested the third time?
7. Did you seek to rest in the Spirit the first time?
8. Did you seek to rest in the Spirit the third time?
9. Have you rested in the Spirit when no one prayed on you?
10. Have you rested in the Spirit while alone?
11. Are you aware of any major healing through resting in the Spirit?
12. Do you feel that resting in the Spirit has been a gift from the Lord for you?
13. Has it helped your prayer life, as far as you know?
14. Has it helped you experience the presence of the Lord in your daily life?
15. Do you think it is appropriate for a Catholic to rest in the Spirit in charismatic services or prayer groups?
16. Would you encourage others to have this experience?
17. Would you like to see it an ordinary part of Catholic life?

Percentages of Yes and No Responses by Category

Male Responses (58 Total)

	1	2	3	4	5	6	7	8	9	10	11	12	13	14	15	16	17
Yes	58	65	18	63	63	60	55	68	43	36	56	93	84	86	94	96	94
No	37	32	81	36	36	25	41	18	56	63	41	5	15	8	0	0	0
Total	95	97	99	99	99	85	96	86	99	99	97	98	99	94	94	96	94

Female Responses (142 Total)

	1	2	3	4	5	6	7	8	9	10	11	12	13	14	15	16	17
Yes	64	61	28	71	68	69	45	61	52	44	53	95	81	87	90	88	85
No	29	36	69	25	29	17	54	28	44	51	42	2	13	4	4	3	4
Total	93	97	97	96	97	86	99	89	96	95	95	97	94	91	94	91	89

Total Responses (200 Total)

	1	2	3	4	5	6	7	8	9	10	11	12	13	14	15	16	17
Yes	62	62	25	69	66	48	48	63	50	41	54	94	82	86	91	90	87
No	31	35	72	28	31	19	50	25	47	54	41	2	13	5	2	2	3
Total	93	97	97	97	97	85	98	88	97	95	95	96	95	91	93	92	90

Physicians

Physician	Possibly Hypnosis or Mass Hysteria	Not Hypnosis or Mass Hysteria	Uncertain	Do not recommend	Recommend testing as Therapeutic	Emotional healing	Physical healing	Spiritual healing	Healing? YES	Healing? NO	Times rested in Spirit	Years in renewal
1			X	X		X	X		X	X	1	6+
2			X			X	X	X	X	X	3-4	6+
3			X			X	X		X	X	10	6+
4			X			X	X		X	X	7-8	6+
5							X			X	2	–
6			X	X					X	X	3	6+
7						X	X				2	6+
8						X	X	X			10	6+
9			X	X		X			X	X	2	6+
10			X						X	X	2	–
11			X						X		2	4
12			X			X					1	6+

Psychotherapists, Psychologists

Possibly Hypnosis or Mass Hysteria	Not Hypnosis or Mass Hysteria	Uncertain	Do not recommend	Recommend resting as Therapeutic	Emotional healing	Physical healing	Spiritual healing	Healing? YES	Healing? NO	Times rested in Spirit	Years in renewal
		X			X	X	X	X	X	50	6+
		X		X	X	X		X		2	3-6
					X	X			X	2	1-3
	X			X	X	X		X	X	5	6+
	X	X			X				?	1	6+
		X						X	X	15	6+
		X	X		X	X		?	?	10	6+
		X						?	X	1	6+
		X			X	X			X	4	6+
		X			X	X		X	X	1-2	3-6

Areas of Interest in Research

In the survey of MD's and psychologists I asked what areas of research on resting in the Spirit they would find of interest. Their responses included:

1. Personality types prone to resting; hysteria and suggestibility studies by someone familiar with psychological issues and charismatic phenomena.

2. Research to determine if there are body changes medically measurable: EEG, EMG, etc. (taking preconceptions and expectations into account).

3. Comparing responses between charismatic and non-Christian clients in a psychotherapeutic setting.

4. Purely descriptive data on personal factors of those who have experienced it. Include socio-economic factors, religious practice, personality, attitude toward the experience, etc. Compare with a similar sample which has not rested in the Spirit. Study "how and where" factors or conditions, looking at where it happens, and with whom leading. An attempt to uncover why "here and now" and not "there and then" could be researched. Results of the resting could also be studied, but then the instrument of measurement would be of maximum importance. Differing conditions under which the resting occurred should be noted (perceived safety or social acceptability factors, etc.). Survey-type research is probably the place to start.

5. Documentable healings, especially physical and addictive, prior to and post resting in the Spirit.

6. Compilation of broader healing experiences among Christians.

7. More personal testimony.

Several researchers in the San Francisco Bay area were questioned about the value of doing brainwave and other scientific studies on individuals as they rest in the Spirit.

Their comments and recommendations are listed below:

1. "Brainwave studies may not be important. I'm skeptical of its usefulness, even if you could get it. Real changes that take place in brainwaves are hard to document. When things in the body change, our understanding is miniscule. There is far too much mythology about the alpha state, for example. Popular understanding is close, but not right. Some people go into the alpha state with music and concentration. A person could go into the alpha state while resting in the Spirit, but it could be because he was fantasizing, or just didn't care."

2. "If you really want to know if there is physiologically something different, I would suggest an EMG monitor because, for quick study, the data has more integrity than brainwaves. There are fewer possible interpretations. This will prove that there is a physical shift. But all you will still prove is that resting in the Spirit brought a person into a quality of relaxation that was deeper than before. Hypnosis will also do this."

3. "The methodology is not important. What is important is, 'Does the practice heal more than another practice? Does the person feel better, psychologically or physically? Does the pain leave? Is life better? Do they feel better about themselves?' This is the real test."

4. RECOMMENDATIONS: "Have well-written stories from people who are open; who ask questions; who want to report, not convince. Address scientific aspects straightforwardly (e.g., perhaps resting in the Spirit and hypnosis share some external aspects, remarking and addressing the fact that science does not replace/displace God. God gives us the phenomena that science studies.) Use anecdotal stories with integrity. Tell their attitude about the experience. Relate the sense of meaning the experience had for them. Collect experiences. Don't try to be scientific."

Remarks Received Regarding This Project

— "Thanks for doing this needed work!"
   Chemical Dependency Therapist
   Minnesota

— "I'm glad you're doing this!"
   Psychologist
   Massachusetts

— "Thank you for the opportunity to share. May the Lord bless this work munificently!"
   MD, Family Practice
   New Jersey

— "I praise God for the powerful gift of resting in the Spirit, and for your courageous use of it!"
   Physician
   Wisconsin

Notes

[1]Rackham Holt, *George Washington Carver* (New York: Doubleday and Company, 1940), pp. 239-240.

[2]Msgr. Vincent Walsh, *Keep the Flame Alive* (Merion Station, Pennsylvania: Key of David Publications, 1987), p. 68.

[3]"Vatican Report on Sects, Cults and New Religious Movements (Origins NC Documentary Service, May 22, 1986, Vol. 16, No. 1), 2:1:3.

[4]Father James Hughes, "God Makes Things Happen," Originally published in *New Covenant* (Steubenville, Ohio, February 1988), pp. 32-34. Reprinted with permission.

[5]Father Robert DeGrandis, S.S.J., *Layperson's Manual for the Healing Ministry* (HOM Books, 108 Aberdeen St., Lowell, Massachusetts 01850, 1973), p. 68.

[6]Francis MacNutt, *The Power to Heal* (Notre Dame, Indiana: Ave Maria Press, 1977), pp. 204-205. Used with permission.

[7]Father George Montague, "Slain in the Spirit — A Biblical Assessment," *Catholic Charismatic* (New York:

Paulist Press, Oct.-Nov. 1977), p. 32. Used with permission.

[8]Father Ralph DiOrio, "Instructional Leaflet on Healing," (Leicester, Massachusetts: Office of the Apostolate of Healing).

[9]Kenneth Hagin, *Why Do People Fall Under the Power?* (Tulsa, Oklahoma: Kenneth Hagin Ministries, 1983), p. 2. Used with permission.

[10]Morton Kelsey, *Discernment* (New York: Paulist Press, 1978), p. 17. Used with permission.

[11]Father Ted Dobson, "The Falling Phenomenon," (Denver, Colorado: private document), 1984.

[12]Thomas Keating, *Open Mind, Open Heart* (Warwick, New York: Amity House, Inc., 1986), p. 6. Used with permission.

[13]Walsh, op. cit.

[14]Sister Linda Koontz, private correspondence (Chariscenter, P.O. Box 1065, Notre Dame, Indiana 46558), 1988.

[15]Kelsey, op. cit., p. 30.

[16]Fr. John Hampsch, CMF, private correspondence (P.O. Box 19100, Los Angeles, California 10019).

[17]St. Augustine, *City of God* (New York: Random House, 1950), pp. 830-831.

[18]E. Allison Peers, *The Complete Works of St. Teresa of Jesus* (Kansas City, MO; Sheed and Ward, 1949), p. 108.

[19]MacNutt, op. cit., pp. 193-197.

[20]"The Sermons and Conferences of John Tauler," trans. by Very Rev. Walter Elliot, C.S.P. (Private printing of 500 copies by Apostolic Mission House, Washington, D.C.: 1910), p. 30.

[21]MacNutt, op. cit., pp. 193-197.

[22]Stanley H. Frodsham, *With Signs Following* (Springfield, Missouri: Gospel Publishing House, 1946). Used with permission.

[23]Kathryn Kuhlman with Jamie Buckingham, *A Glimpse Into Glory* (Plainfield, New Jersey: Logos International, 1979), pp. 88-92. Used with permission.

[24]Charles and Frances Hunter, *Supernatural Horizons,* Kingwood, Texas: Hunter Books, 1983), pp. 128-133. Used with permission.

[25]Fr. John Hampsch, op. cit.

[26]Fr. Robert DeGrandis, op. cit., p. 68.

[27]Fr. Ralph DiOrio, *A Miracle to Proclaim* (New York: Doubleday and Co., 1984), pp. 16-19, 32, 41-42, 55. Used with permission.

[28]Rene Laurentin, *Miracles in El Paso?* (Ann Arbor, Michigan: Servant Publications, 1982), pp. 104-105, 107-108. Used with permission.

[29]Ann and Barry Ulanov, *Religion and the Unconscious* (Philadelphia, Pennsylvania: Westminster Press, Louisville, Kentucky, 1975), p. 22. Used with permission.

[30]Sister Francis Clare, SSND, personal correspondence (St. Rita's Convent, 6023 West Lincoln, West Allis, Wisconsin).

[31] Al and Patti Mansfield, "Questions and Answers," New Covenant (Steubenville, Ohio, March 1986), p. 29. Used with permission.

[32] Leon Joseph Cardinal Suenens, *A Controversial Phenomenon, Resting in the Spirit* (Dublin, Ireland: Veritas Publications 1987).

[33] Father Richard Bain, private correspondence (San Francisco, California, 1987).

[34] Father George Maloney, "How to Understand and Evaluate the Charismatics' Newest Experience: 'Slaying in the Spirit.' " Reprinted with permission from the publishers of *Crux of the News,* 75 Champlain St., Albany, New York 12204. No further reprinting without authorization.

[35] MacNutt, op. cit., p. 218.

[36] Dorothea DeGrandis Sudol, personal correspondence (108 Aberdeen St., Lowell, Massachusetts 01850).

[37] MacNutt, op. cit., p. 214.

[38] DeGrandis, op. cit., p. 68-69.

[39] MacNutt, op. cit., p. 223.

[40] Frodsham, op. cit., p. 94.

For more of Fr. Robert DeGrandis' books or tapes, contact:

Charismatic Renewal Services
P.O. Box 4456
South Bend, IN 46634